The Diary, and Life, of
William Byrd II of Virginia,
1674–1744

The Diary, and Life, of William Byrd II of Virginia, 1674–1744

Kenneth A. Lockridge

W·W· NORTON & COMPANY
New York · London

Published for the
Institute of Early American History and Culture
Williamsburg, Virginia

Published simultaneously in Canada
by Penguin Books Canada Ltd,
2801 John Street, Markham, Ontario L3R 1B4

First published as a Norton paperback 1988
by arrangement with
The University of North Carolina Press

Library of Congress Cataloging-in-Publication Data

Lockridge, Kenneth A.
   The diary and life of William Byrd II of Virginia,
1674–1744.

Reprint. Originally published: Chapel Hill:
Published for the Institute of Early American
History and Culture by The University of
North Carolina Press, © 1987.

   Bibliography: p.
   Includes index.
      1. Byrd, William, 1674–1744—Diaries. 2. Virginia—
Social life and customs—Colonial period, ca. 1600–1775.
3. Plantation owners—Virginia—Diaries. I. Institute
of Early American History and Culture (Williamsburg, Va.)
II. Title.
F229.B978   1987   975.5′02′0924 [B]

ISBN 0-393-95682-2

W. W. Norton & Company, Inc., 500 Fifth Avenue, New York, N.Y. 10110
W. W. Norton & Company Ltd., 37 Great Russell Street, London, WC1B 3NU

1 2 3 4 5 6 7 8 9 0

To my son Kris

and to the memory of

Stephen Botein

Preface*

William Byrd has been something of an enigma to American historians. The basic facts of his life, as they might be entered in an encyclopedia, are clear enough. Born in Virginia in 1674, and educated in England, he returned to Virginia in 1705 and helped his planter brethren seize effective control of the colony's affairs from their royal governor, Sir Alexander Spotswood, in the years 1710–1722. Byrd's aspirations went higher still, and he spent most of the years 1714 to 1726 in London pursuing his ambition to be made royal governor of Virginia. But in the latter year he returned to Virginia to take up once again his position on the Council of State there and to accept his role as one of the more prominent members of the colony's indigenous political elite. Thereafter Byrd and his fellow members of that elite steered Virginia with only modest interference by the Board of Trade in England or the king's governors in the colony. Byrd died in 1744.

For most of his life William Byrd was also a diarist and man of letters, and as such he probably wrote more than any colonial American save Cotton Mather. But because his writings give only fleeting access to the man, his inner life remains virtually unexplored. This is an effort to explore that life. It is an attempt to suggest how early Virginia's culture shaped Byrd's personality, and how that personality in turn found expression in the genres available to him in the transatlantic world of the early eighteenth century. Created by his culture, he finally became an instrument shaping that culture in turn, during the golden age of the tidewater gentry just before midcentury. It is also a story of the price one provincial paid for reaching a late maturity which coincided with the first maturity of his class in Virginia. And it is the story of his efforts to preserve that class and its culture in the face of a future he sensed coming.

This story is only a beginning. Many of Byrd's manuscripts are cryptic. Many are only tentatively dated. Many others seem not to have survived at all. The other sources waiting in the archives of the United States and Great Britain will surely reveal still other William Byrds. Better stories will be told about this man's life as time goes on. This is just a first exploration of the possibilities of a remarkable life. Seen from within, however, it glows with meanings that need to be uttered. While any of those meanings may be revised, they demonstrate the range of William Byrd's life, as of any life, and of his culture, as of any culture. Such a biography is ultimately an exploration of the limits of culture.

It is not a psychobiography, it is not quite ethnography, it is not a final biography. It is a story of events, of personality, of texts, of new events, of a maturing personality, of mature texts. It is the story of a man who struggled free of the damage his circumstances and culture did to him to become an actor in history, shaping the culture of his homeland within the limitations which his personality, and time, imposed on him. I admit that I hope it is true.

Contents

Illustrations

Chronology of the Life of William Byrd II

1674	Born March 28, son of Mary Horsmanden Byrd and William Byrd I, himself a planter-trader in Virginia and the son of a London goldsmith.
1676	Sent away for safety during Bacon's Rebellion.
1681	Sent to England to attend Felsted School.
1690	Leaves Felsted.
	Serves brief apprenticeship in the Netherlands.
1692	Enters Middle Temple for legal training.
	Becomes protégé of Sir Robert Southwell
	member of Royal Society
	agent for Virginia House of Burgesses
	man about town.
1696	Rejected for a position with Board of Trade.
	Returns briefly to Virginia; elected to House of Burgesses.
1697	Returns to London.
1704	William Byrd I dies.
	Writes self-portrait, "Inamorato L'Oiseaux"?
1705	Returns to inherit father's estates in Virginia.
1706	Marries Lucy Parke.
1709	Takes father's place on Council of State in Virginia.
	Unsuccessfully seeks governorships of Virginia and Maryland.
	Begins secret diary.
1710	Infant son dies.
	Alexander Spotswood arrives as governor of Virginia.
1714	In England to challenge Spotswood's policies and to unseat Spotswood; also to settle the debts of his father-in-law, which he has assumed.

1716	Lucy joins him in London, where she dies of smallpox.
1718	Fails to win hand of wealthy "Sabina."
1719	Ordered home by Board of Trade to make peace with Spotswood.
1719–1721	In Virginia, receives warm reception from colleagues and neighbors courts burgesses talks with his slaves.
1722–1726	Back in London.
1722	Spotswood removed as governor of Virginia.
1724	Marries Maria Taylor.
1726	Returns with new family to Virginia.
1726ff.	Leads fight against Colonial Debts Act. William Gooch governor of Virginia (1726–1747).
1728	Runs dividing line with North Carolina.
1729	Plans to build new mansion house at Westover and to import German-Swiss settlers for "Land of Eden."
1729–1736	Writes two histories of the dividing line.
1736–1744	At home at Westover.
1744	Dies August 26, president of Council of State solvent (his creditors bankrupt).

The Diary, and Life, of William Byrd II of Virginia, 1674–1744

I

These books are in code. One has ended up at the Huntington Library in California, one at the University of North Carolina Library, and one at the Virginia Historical Society in Richmond. Most have never been found. We do not know with certainty when William Byrd II began writing them or why, though it was probably shortly after his return to Virginia in 1705 to assume his father's estates and role. We know only that he kept them in an obscure form of shorthand and seems to have written in them almost every day of his life, at least from the time he was thirty-five, in 1709, until shortly before his death in 1744 at the age of seventy. In the surviving diaries, for 1709–1712, 1717–1721, and 1739–1741, virtually every word is in shorthand and not more than thirty-two days in these eleven years went by without an entry made that night, the next morning or rarely, a day or two later.[1]

Byrd seems to have used shorthand as a code, not just as a means of writing swiftly. The average entry is less than one hundred words, so little time was saved by shorthand. He appears generally to have written up the previous days during his long, leisurely mornings, when time was ample. There are, quite simply, things in the diary which no eighteenth-century gentleman would have wanted known about himself. "Rogered my wife" was not the stuff of drawing-room conversation in the eighteenth century any more than today. Many such sexual revelations are confided to the diary. Still other intimate exposures, of dreams, of political ambitions, occur rarely but spontaneously throughout the books. Short-

hand gave Byrd the freedom to utter such things, though
he seldom took full advantage of it to unburden himself at
length. It is also plain that in a wider sense the man never
intended his diary to be known by others. Its clipped, intimate tone makes it unmistakably a private set of reminders
for the writer alone. Byrd's intentions might further be read
in the fact that the shorthand was a rare form, and that he
retained no copy of the book from which he had learned it,
William Mason's *La plume volante* (1707), in his immense
library. Neither he nor his family or friends ever mentioned
the diary's existence. Nor did he make provision for its preservation. It was scattered, and no part of it was rediscovered
until 1939.[2] As is generally acknowledged, it is a "Secret
Diary."

Rediscovered, the coded volumes stand in octavo. They
are compact. One, for example, measures exactly 6⅜ by
3¾ inches. Though they are bound in leather, they are simple
books, of the sort still referred to as notebooks. They are of
the sort also used at the time as commonplace books, or as
letter books, or by schoolboys as copybooks. Now, of course,
their bindings are shattered and some of the pages torn. The
oblong blocks of their daily entries march steadily down the
rectilinear page. Within each entry, the neat cursive marks
are set into short sentences by rigid vertical slashes, like ex-
clamation points. The whole gives an inscrutably military
appearance.[3] Compulsively kept for four decades, this diary
is in code. It seems to dare us to know what it stands for.

Translated into English letters, the diary is still encoded.
Every day from 1709 on, with appalling regularity, Byrd recorded chiefly only that he rose at five (later six), read in
Hebrew and Greek, said his prayers, ate breakfast, "danced"
(exercised), did some accounts or letters, read Latin, ate dinner shortly after midday, did business and visited or was visited, possibly read still more Latin and Greek, looked after
his plantation and slaves, possibly walked with his wife, said
his prayers, and "had good health, good thoughts, and good

humor, thanks be to God Almighty." There are sometimes small breaches of this sequence of behaviors or occasionally one or two of the most standard items in the routine are omitted. "Dancing" is never done every day. Interlaced within this repertoire are sporadic sentences on events or the weather and intermittent brief sexual revelations, dreams, or visions.[4] The sequence in its early, fullest form can be seen in the three entries for July 7, 8, and 9, 1709.

> 7. I rose at 5 o'clock and read a chapter in Hebrew and some Greek in Josephus. I said my prayers and ate milk for breakfast. I danced my dance, and settled my accounts. I read some Latin. It was extremely hot. I ate stewed mutton for dinner. In the afternoon it began to rain and blow very violently so that it blew down my fence. It likewise thundered. In all the time I have been in Virginia I never heard it blow harder. I read Latin again and Greek in Homer. In the evening we took a walk in the garden. I said my prayers and had good health, good humor and good thoughts, thanks be to God Almighty.

> 8. I rose at 5 o'clock and read a chapter in Hebrew and some Greek in Josephus. I said my prayers and ate milk for breakfast. I danced my dance. I read some Latin. Tom returned from Williamsburg and brought me a letter from Mr. Bland which told me the wine came out very well. I ate nothing but pudding for dinner. In the afternoon I read some more Latin and Greek in Homer. Then I took a walk about the plantation. I said my prayers and had good health, good thoughts, and good humor, thanks be to God Almighty.

> 9. I rose at 5 o'clock and read two chapters in Hebrew and some Greek in Josephus. I said my prayers and ate milk and apples for breakfast with Captain Wilcox who called here this morning. I danced my dance. I wrote a

Pages from William Byrd's secret diary.
Courtesy of The Huntington Library, San Marino,
California.

July 1710.

15.

16.

17.

18.

19.

letter to England and read some Latin. I ate roast chicken
for dinner. In the afternoon I saluted my wife and took a
nap. I read more Latin and Greek in Homer. Then I took
a walk about the plantation. I neglected to say my prayers. I had good health, good thoughts, and good humor,
thanks be to God Almighty.

As Byrd aged, the routine, and the entries, grew shorter,
but the form was basically unchanged.[5] Byrd's very behavior
was encoded. Or, his memory of each day's behavior, written
into his diary, was rendered into a fairly rigid and obsessively
repetitive behavioral code. Plainly, what the diary describes
are the expected behaviors of an eighteenth-century gentleman repeated and obsessively reviewed. Its shorthand code
simply hides a behavioral code so rigid and unrevealing that
it scarcely need have been put in shorthand. It is typical that
Byrd chose to put such behavior, as well as his occasional
small revelations of self, into the shorthand code.

A third code lies in the language of the diary. The events
which fall between the parts of the behavioral routine and in
the end that routine itself are cast in the emotional code of
the eighteenth-century gentleman, emphasizing moderation,
balance, and acceptance in all things. Byrd could have taken
that code straight from the pages of his *Tatler* or *Spectator*.
When vicissitudes arose, when his tobacco was lost at sea,
when he quarreled with his wife, Byrd's classic reply was
"God's will be done." Even faced with his infant son's death,
"God gives and God takes away; blessed be the name of
God."[6] In Byrd, such Christian submission was always associated with a conviction that moderation and balance and acceptance were the root of civilized behavior. God may or may
not have cared whether Byrd had "good thoughts, good humor, and good health" every night of his life, but it was vital
to William Byrd's image of himself as a social being that
he regard the world with this profound equanimity come
what may.

Byrd was apologetic when he failed to maintain his composure: "had good thoughts, good humor, but indifferent health," or "good health, good thoughts, but indifferent humor, thanks be to God Almighty." But usually within a day he could approve of his humor again.[7] The achievement of equanimity made him proud, as on May 6, 1709, when Byrd heard that a ship carrying much of his tobacco crop had gone down in Margate Roads: "I had good health, good thoughts, and good humor, notwithstanding my misfortune, thanks be to God Almighty." Particularly with respect to his wife Lucy, Byrd had to struggle visibly to hold his composure, and so he was all the more proud of his success. "My wife and I had another foolish quarrel about my saying she listened on the top of the stairs, which I suspected [another example of Byrd's concern for secrecy], in jest. However, I bore it with patience and she came soon after and begged my pardon."[8] God did not directly enter into this last example, only what the eighteenth century called civility.

There was, however, no conflict between God and civility for many such gentlemen as William Byrd. They had an explicit model for combining the two in Richard Steele's *The Christian Hero*, published in 1701. In this essay Steele abandoned the Stoics' faith in reason alone and rested the composure and benevolence of the gentleman in Christian faith. It is this exact philosophy which soon permeated the pages of Steele's *Tatler*, which Byrd read, and which by 1709 was everywhere embodied in the Virginian's diary.[9] The problem is that Byrd's emotions, rendered into this code of equanimity, are often so deeply encoded as to lose all further content. Byrd virtually never goes on to explain his emotions in the diary. What mattered was that he record mastering them.

Thus, the diary is triply encoded. Once in a literal code, a rare shorthand. Once in that it describes chiefly the expected behaviors of an eighteenth-century gentleman, repeated and obsessively reviewed. Once again in that all entries are rendered in terms of that emotional moderation, balance, and acceptance which, with learning and right behavior, defined that era's gentleman. From the modern reader's point of view, a more elegant form of self-constriction has never been devised. The last two of these codes act so powerfully as a filter that they threaten to hide everything else of William Byrd from sight. Or rather, the behavioral routine and the emotional restraint are so deeply engrained that they raise the possibility that beneath these codes there *was* nothing to hide. William Byrd was his secrecy, his routine, his restraint.

Byrd's diary is a far cry from the better-known diary of Samuel Pepys, another peripheral gentleman. Beneath Pepys's shorthand, which like Byrd's was a code aimed at secrecy, lies a wealth of varied behavior amply described. Social interactions are richly documented in fat paragraphs. Pepys's revelations of himself are equally well developed and are at times almost embarrassingly frank. It is easy to see why he was scarcely considered a gentleman. It was not only his middle-class background which cost him this title with his betters, it was as surely his scurrying frankness about all things most of all himself. All diarists are studied, but Pepys, like John Evelyn or Dudley Ryder, poured out a wealth of information and reflection while arranging himself by whatever subtler inner codes he used to order his teeming existence as that existence spilled out onto the pages of his diary. Byrd's diary is also quite unlike that of his near contemporary in Virginia, the Reverend Robert Rose.[10] Rose's diary is in English letters, and while its entries are likewise short, they are straightforward descriptions of days more varied than Byrd's. Rose's narrative is taken up with the changing details of his business rather than with the largely unconscious regularities of his life. These details are recorded briefly but in a relatively unstudied voice. By comparison, Byrd's diary threatens constantly to have no content beyond its forms.

There is in fact probably no English-language diary of the eighteenth century so deeply encoded as William Byrd's. Some diaries were kept in a secret shorthand, as with Pepys's;

many also show inadvertent evidence of a de facto daily or
weekly routine, as does Rose's; and many show an emotional
restraint typical of the age, as Evelyn sometimes evinces explicitly and Rose achieves by silence. But no known diary
combines a secret shorthand, a self-consciously ritualistic
behavioral routine compulsively observed, and an elabo-
rately studied cultivation of emotional restraint into the
triad of powerful self-encodements found here. Possibly no
English-language diary of this period fully achieves even the
latter two of these three encodements to the degree found in
Byrd's diary.[11]

The codified nature of the diary explains why the creation
which most makes William Byrd famous, his diary, is also
the reason historians have had trouble understanding him.
For Virginia historians of past generations, it has been enough
that Byrd was a symbol for the rich accomplishments of the
plantation gentry. They did not require more depth from the
man. In later years a fascination with English diaries has led
scholars of this subject to turn to the American William Byrd
for comparisons, inevitably to be repulsed. Pepys's most recent editor, William Matthews, could only observe "that it is
possible for a diarist to be historically minded, scientific,
honest, accurate, careful, copious, even to write in shorthand, and yet to be considerably dull, is evident from the
diary (1709–12) of an eminent American colonist, Richard
Byrd of Westover, Virginia." Dull enough, evidently, to have
his name mistaken! In *Private Chronicles: A Study of English Diaries,* Robert Fothergill expresses a similar reaction.

> As an extreme contrast to [Dudley] Ryder's diary, . . .
> there stands the *London Diary* . . . of William Byrd of
> Virginia. . . . It promises at first glance to add just that
> element of hearty candour and pleasure . . . which would
> allow it to share with Ryder's the joint-inheritance of
> Pepys. But . . . Byrd cannot rise above the most mechani-
> cal record of his actions. He . . . resorts to plain sum-

maries of each day's doings so nearly identical as to give
the impression of a simply automatic habit. Even his
sexual candour . . . turns out to be a dull regimen. . . .[12]

To Lawrence Stone, student of the English aristocracy,
Byrd's cryptic record has been equally a source of frustration.
Comparing the Virginian to equally well recorded British diarists, such as Pepys and Boswell, Stone can only observe
in vexation that Byrd was cold and unrevealing. Michael
Zuckerman has attempted to solve the problem by taking
Byrd's diary at its word: if Byrd records simply that his son
died, then he was not much moved by the death; if Byrd visited or was visited x number of times, then he was an obsessive visitor. In desperation, another student has resorted
to a kind of positional analysis, in which tiny variations in
Byrd's rigid routine are used as clues to his feelings.[13] By brilliant application, these historians and others have dented the
armor of the diary in intriguing ways. But the Byrd of the
diary remains, as he seems to have intended, secret.
    William Byrd seems little more revealed in his other texts.
His letters are generally classic eighteenth-century business
communications. Political opinions are rarely expressed and
run true to form for his class and place. Family is usually
rendered into brief formulae. His more famous writings
are often very studied pieces indeed, his love letters sometimes a flood of clichés, his portraits of contemporaries
equally abstract whether bitter or fawning, and his histories
of the dividing line between Virginia and North Carolina are
therefore sometimes thought to be the too painfully self-
conscious creations of a provincial aping his betters in London.[14] The main issue has been to assess Byrd's talent in these
pieces, not what they reveal about the man and his creations
together.
    All Byrd's texts, then, are the enigma. They explain why
one of the best-documented men in colonial America is still
to us no more than the Virginia planter-politician of the great

age, known chiefly in terms of his external achievements. The texts are so enigmatic that they make it inevitable that any biography of William Byrd II will be a speculative biography, resting on unproven theories and on subtle judgments of tone. No historian can escape from this necessity.

The curious thing in all of this is the nearly universal agreement on William Byrd's personality, which I regard as one key to why the diary is so encoded and also as one key to decoding both the diary and his life. While I go farther here than some previous treatments of Byrd, this sketch of his personality does not substantially conflict with existing observations. When he was seven, Byrd was sent by his ambitious middle-class father to England for a gentleman's education at Felsted School. He saw his father only twice and his mother but once again. When he emerges from school into our (i.e., recorded) experience in the London of the 1690s, at twenty-two or so, he is recognizably the brittle, studied person he was to remain in some degree all his life. His love letters and satires of this and subsequent decades are almost hysterical parodies of genres better practiced by others. By his own admission, in a self-portrait rewritten in 1721 but probably begun earlier, he is uncontrollably foolish when confronted with something he really wants, usually a wealthy and preferably a titled bride. He is scrupulous in doing his father's bidding as agent for the Council in Virginia, on which his father sits, and he has begun a lifelong effort to outdo or at least to match his father's achievements, an effort which will end in his career being in many respects a duplicate of his father's. He shows as well his father's horror of debt. The difference between the two men is that what in the father was straightforward seventeenth-century ambition, blunt and direct though adequately polite, is in the son a nervous pursuit of ambition with excessive politesse.[15]

If this is our man, in his twenties, thirties, and forties in the years 1690–1720, as he emerges into the record, first of his letters, then of the colonial bureaucracy, the courts, the

Royal Society, and finally, after 1709, of his diary, then the
diary becomes far less cryptic. Its very crypticity becomes
expressive.

II

Any reconstruction of Byrd's personality is speculative, but in retrospect the central event in Byrd's life appears to have been his being sent from Virginia in 1681, at
the age of seven, via his mother's relatives to attend Felsted
School in England.[16] It was a shock which he appears to have
explained to himself, as his father may have, as a necessity.
Adjusting to this shock in an environment in which he was a
stranger and seems to have been isolated from close relationships, the boy shaped the brittle personality seen so vividly
in the texts of his early adult life. It was a variant on the personality of the eighteenth-century gentleman, the product of
difficult conditions, and it helps unlock the texts he created.
His texts, in turn, will show that personality eventually
reaching maturity.

Young Byrd was sent to England to fulfill his father's ambitions. Years later, in a moment of great uncertainty just as he
began keeping his diary, the grown William Byrd II would dig
up his dead father's body and seek advice in its "wasted coun-
tenance."[17] He would find no answer there, but his painful
query to the dead man suggests that Byrd's relationship to his
father, who had sent him to England as a boy, was to become
central to his life and that his father is the place to begin relating that life. William Byrd I was an ambitious man of
middle-class origins with an eye for the main chance.[18] He
had made his real money in the Indian trade, and in 1676,
when shut out of it, he joined the "rabble" around Nathaniel
Bacon in rebelling against Governor William Berkeley. In the
course of the rebellion Byrd senior seems to have undergone
an opportune conversion. He emerged at the victorious gover-

nor's right hand and was soon appointed a member of the royal
Council, the upper house of the colonial Virginia legislature.
He eventually moved downriver from his initial trading post
above the falls of the James River into the rich tidewater tobacco country nearer the seat of government in Jamestown.
He would rebel no more, though like most councillors, he
would continue to bridle at all restraints suggested by the
succession of officers sent by the king to govern Virginia. In
1673 William Byrd I had married Mary Horsmanden Filmer,
a lady of gentle birth and the widow of a gentleman settler
who had sickened and died in Virginia. Now, in 1681, just five
years after the rising of the "rabble" during Bacon's Rebellion
and in the midst of his newfound respectability as a councillor, William Byrd I decided to send his only son to his
wife's Cavalier family in England for an education at their old
school, Felsted.

Simultaneously other planters of this half-polished first
generation concluded that their sons needed an English education. Bacon's Rebellion was probably one spur which drove
them on, as they still had Nathaniel Bacon's contemptuous
judgment on their sort ringing in their ears.

> Let us trace these men in Authority and Favour to whose
> hands the dispensation of the Countries wealth has been
> commited; let us observe the sudden Rise of their Es-
> tates composed with the Quality in which they first en-
> tered this Country Or the Reputation they have held
> here amongst wise and discerning men, And lett us see
> wither their extractions and Education have not bin vile,
> And by what pretence of learning and vertue they could
> [come] soe soon into Imployments of so great Trust and
> consequence.

Bacon and his rebellious followers had gone down to defeat,
but not before the lesson had been learned that even the best
of the new-minted Virginia "gentlemen," those who had
rallied around Governor Berkeley, were no real gentlemen

at all, and could not command respect when political tur-
bulence arose. For that matter, by the time the rebellion was
over, these would-be gentlemen scarcely commanded respect
from Berkeley either, and against their advice he hanged
many of the leaders of the rebellion. The implication of this
recent experience was that the planters thought that an English education would help their sons to control both the
"rabble" of freed white servants who had joined Bacon in his
rebellion and the "tyrannical" officers sent by the king to
govern Virginia. Personal ambition spoke here as well, for by
English tradition any tradesman who settled on enough land
and educated his heir sufficiently could see his son raise the
family to gentle status. Everything in William Byrd I's career
pointed to a hunger for such status even without considering
the mockery he and his followers had received from rabble
beneath and governors above. He never stated his motives,
but he supervised their fulfillment in his son.[19]

The seven-year-old boy came across the sea in 1681 with a
heavy weight of expectation on him. He found little support.
Most probably his father sent his young son through Perry
and Lane, his English merchants, to his mother's father,
Warham Horsmanden of Purleigh in Essex, with the words
"My little son William comes herewith, to whom I shall not
doubt your kindnesse." His younger sisters were consigned
with these words soon after. Young Byrd went immediately
on to Felsted School. It was a small school, of at most several
dozen scholars, most local "charity" lads with a sprinkling
of "gentleman" scholars, many sons from the nearby household of the Riche family, sometime earls of Warwick, and
two tutors, the chief of whom was the aged Christopher
Glasscock. The school was just entering a long period of de-
cline, especially after 1685 when the Riches ceased their
close patronage, so the school continued to be housed simply,
in the upper floor of a Tudor guildhall in the village of
Felsted. This barnlike space was known as the Old School
Room. The boys boarded here and there in the village as space

was available. During the years he was there, 1681–1690, Byrd was increasingly the ward of his maternal uncle, Daniel Horsmanden. Little is known about this uncle, save that by 1691 he was complaining about the trouble and expense of supervising the Byrd children. Byrd senior was forced to place his children elsewhere. From later evidence, his son seems never to have formed a close relationship either with his maternal grandfather or with his complaining uncle.[20]

Because young William saw his father only twice again in his life, his father became a distant presence for him, and an occasional voice urging him on. In the first years the older Byrds' chief contact with their children seems to have been limited to "our blessings to our children" appended to Byrd senior's business letters to Warham and Daniel Horsmanden. While at Felsted the boy wrote to his father occasionally to report his progress at school, but only a few such letters are referred to in William Byrd I's letter book. The same letter book contains two replies from the father, both occasioned by letters from the boy, in a process of exchanging letters across the Atlantic which meant that the father's reply came perhaps six months after the son's letter. The chief import of the letter sent to the eleven-year-old schoolboy in 1685 was to "improve your time, and bee carefull to serve God as you ought, without which you cannot expect to doe well here or hereafter." Five years later in 1690, as Byrd left the school, the father was "heartily glad to hear you had your health so well, and hope to find you have improved your time so, that you may answer the expectation of all your friends." Byrd senior then confirmed his son's request to be apprenticed temporarily to Perry and Lane in London, and reminded him to be "mindfull of your duty to heaven, and then you may be assured God will bless you in all your undertakings." There was, however, fondness in the father's tone at the end: "Pray when you come to London let me hear from you often, for there you cannot want oppertunitys. Your mother is in health and gives you her blessing, your sister Mary is well and all

friends. God bless thee in all thy ways is the hearty prayer of
thy affectionate father WB."[21]

If these were Byrd's only communications from his father
while at Felsted, or if their brevity is typical of the letters he
received, how great a contrast this must have been to the personal contact other sons had with their fathers while at the
school. Most of the "gentleman scholars" at Felsted were
from nearby Surrey or Essex and could see their families frequently. Such proximity meant that their fathers could more
easily monitor their progress by letter as well.[22] By contrast,
William Byrd I's advice to his son to "improve" was not much
to go on. The hearty but distant voice of his father, which
his letters elicited, associated God with success in the boy's
mind and left no doubt, whatever its crypticity otherwise,
that "improvement" was to be defined in worldly terms. Exactly what "improvement" meant, however, was never made
clear save by the substance of his father's letters to Daniel
Horsmanden enlisting the latter's help in obtaining royal
office in Virginia. The purpose of the elder Byrd's only visit to
England, in 1687–1688, was to nail down the place of auditor
and receiver of the royal revenues in Virginia, worth perhaps
500 pounds a year. His greetings to his son in letters and his
one greeting in person were, typically, incidental to the father's pursuit of office.[23] The elder William Byrd's actions
were the only indication given his son of where improvement
was to lead. As instruction, it was a bit thin, though it was a
lesson not to be lost on the son.

Plainly, from the fact of his consignment to the Horsmandens and their school, young William was to receive first of
all a gentleman's education.[24] But he found no living model
with which to fill in the details of what a gentleman was, to
help him in conforming to this imperative of his distant father. Nothing in his later writings indicates that his aged
grandfather and impatient uncle became the "significant
others" on whom young William Byrd could model the details of a gentleman's life in the immediate pursuit of his fa-

ther's purposes. Christopher Glasscock, rector of Felsted, was satisfied with the boy's progress, but Byrd seems never to have formed a memorable relationship with him, either. In any event, Glasscock was infirm, and died in 1690, just as Byrd left school, and so provided no continuing guidance. No man emerges from these years to whom Byrd referred with affectionate respect or indeed at all later in his life. From all the evidence, young Byrd was not to find a living mentor until his father introduced him by letter to Sir Robert Southwell in the middle 1690s, when Byrd was more than twenty years old.[25]

Nor does Byrd seem to have found a model in his school chums at Felsted. It is said that young Sir John Perceval, later Lord Egmont, and a lifelong acquaintance, was at Felsted with Byrd. But neither ever mentioned it.[26] The friendship with Perceval was chiefly a result of Byrd's later attachment to Sir Robert Southwell, to whom Perceval was a nephew and a more distinguished protégé. That friendship was preserved in later life because Perceval, as Egmont, became a political power in England and so useful to Byrd.[27] Only one school fellow is positively identified in Byrd's later writings, "my old school fellow" Dr. William Cocke, who showed up in Virginia in 1710 as physician and advisor to the new governor, Sir Alexander Spotswood. As will be seen, Byrd's relationship with Cocke was initially very tense indeed. Judging from the diary, their relationship never included any reminiscence about Felsted.[28] These may have been very lonely years for the young Virginian. They certainly became silent ones. In a lifetime of diaries, letters, and other writings, the mention of "my old school fellow Cocke" is the only reference to Byrd's school days.

There may have been a reason for Byrd's evident isolation at school and for his later silence. After leaving school in 1690 he served as an apprentice with Perry and Lane and in 1692 entered the Middle Temple to read law. When he did so, he identified himself in the book listing new entrants as the "son and heir apparent of William Byrd of Cree Church, London, Esq." He was his father's son and, in emphasizing his father's English origins, was casting himself emphatically as an Englishman. Safe in this status, he would enjoy the years at Middle Temple immensely. Late in life he would reminisce with Benjamin Lynde, a Massachusetts native and good friend from the Middle Temple days—his first good friend in England and, significantly, a colonial—on their high jinks with "the jades."[29] But both his identification of himself as an Englishman with no reference to his colonial status, and his choice of a fellow colonial for his first true friendship untainted by clientage after eleven years in England suggest that Byrd had encountered rejections at school on account of his colonial origins. After school Byrd hid those origins, but sought his best friend among his own kind. And indeed Byrd may from the beginning have been out of place among the local "charity lads" at Felsted, while the "gentleman scholars" were sons of gentry from the nearby region with networks and contacts of their own. Neither group could have known much about Virginia, save perhaps, as educated Englishmen and women sometimes did, to wonder if English was spoken there at all. Such a rejection would help explain his failure to find close friendships while at school. Certainly, he was later to characterize himself as sensitive to slights, and the slight he most sought to explain away or to rise above was any aspersion on his colonial origins.[30] The inscription in the Middle Temple book may express the reason for Byrd's loneliness and for his silence about his school years. In later years in Virginia he did not send his own son away to England to school, excusing this on account of a tenderheartedness in his second wife, but the tenderheartedness was all too clearly in himself.[31] He could not send his son away as he had been sent.

Sent away by his parents to the hard benches of the Old School Room in the attic of the guildhall at Felsted, urged on by his distant father, and without significant attachments,

The Old School Room at Felsted School.
Photograph courtesy of Mr. Michael Craze.

what young William Byrd does seem to have done most in his
school years was learn languages and read books. The Greek
and Latin, possibly also the Hebrew, French, and Italian, he
read all his life were learned as far as can be known at school.
These languages gave him access to many of the books he
later acquired for his large library, and he used both the languages and the books for the rest of his life. Reading in solitude, which he spent much of his later life doing, was possibly learned here. More significantly, some of the books in his
library at his death were seventeenth-century editions and
were very probably acquired during the 1680s or after leaving
school but before his return to Virginia in 1705. Among these
were Peacham's *Compleat Gentleman,* and works by Francis
Bacon, Thomas Hobbes, John Locke, Richard Allestree, Sir
William Temple, and Richard Steele, all of whom were tutors
of and models for the Christian gentleman of the late seventeenth century.[32] It was indisputably from these experiences
more than from personal relationships that the boy shaped
his personality. Books were all he brought with him out of
his school years, books and the personality they helped him
shape.

Exactly what happened is not clear, but it could have run
something like this. William Byrd had to explain to himself
the shock of his exile. He could only explain it as his father
may have, as a necessity. If, in rowdy and rebellious Virginia,
the potentially gentle family his father was creating was to
acquire the polish and influence which would enable it to
consolidate its gains—the polish to impress the turbulent
populace, the influence to obtain from the crown positions
of profit and power preferably within Virginia but if need be
anywhere in the empire—then William Byrd II must be sent
to his mother's Cavalier family and to their school. Measur-
ing up to this goal became young William's way of explaining
to himself the hurt of a rejection, his exile, which was no less
profound for being somewhat in keeping with the mores of

gentle Englishmen then and now. The rejection may have been redoubled by ridicule from his schoolmates about his colonial origins. He was truly a boy "in-between," with no real home. To "improve," as his father put it, meant first of all to be what Felsted School was intended to create, a gentleman. Later, it would mean the pursuit of office. Yet neither in his mother's family nor at Felsted School did Byrd grow close to anyone who could embody for him what a gentleman was. His uncle was irritable, his rector old and possibly distant, his classmates did not become close friends. So he turned to books.

At Felsted School, then, sometime in the years 1681–1690 when Byrd was seven to sixteen years old, and continuing to an indeterminate degree into the years immediately thereafter, he learned to read Greek, Latin, and Hebrew. He learned to "dance his dance." He read such things as Peacham's *Compleat Gentleman*, Allestree's *Whole Duty of Man*, and Sir William Temple's essays extolling classical learning. He may have read Francis Bacon's essay "On the Advancement of Learning" or "Of Travel," in which Bacon recommends to young men traveling that they keep a journal. Hungry to show that his exile had a purpose, eager to measure up to the intentions of and so to draw closer to his absent father (and mother), wanting to shine in the eyes of his maternal uncle and cousins, the boy seized on the project of becoming a perfect gentleman. But because his drive was fueled by profound rejection, as son and as colonial, and because, lacking a significant other to embody the role as a set of living metaphors, he learned it through books alone, William Byrd II could never be sure he was a gentleman, and his conception of the role was rigid and narrow. It is this William Byrd who first emerges into the texts of 1690–1720 and who never entirely disappears.[33]

During or just after his school years the young William Byrd may have acquired not only the artificial project of be-

coming a perfect gentleman from books, and the personality
which went with it, but also the exact prescriptions for a
gentleman's behavior which he was eventually so compulsively to review in his diary. Of all the books the boy might
have read while at school, or which the Felsted curriculum
might have digested into a gentleman's code of behavior
that the boy in turn could have adopted rigidly to guide his
project, two stand out. These are Sir Thomas Elyot's *The
Boke Named the Governour*, first published in the sixteenth
century but still much discussed in the seventeenth, and
Richard Brathwait's *The English Gentleman*, issued at London in 1630 and reissued thereafter.[34] The behavioral routines in Byrd's diary and indeed the idea of a diary itself can
be found in the pages of these two books alone, as can Byrd's
early prose style.

Both books speak of aspiring to be a perfect gentleman, and
Brathwait has a large section on "Perfection," emphasizing
that perfection in a gentleman is gradually attainable. He defines such an enterprise as "improvement." Brathwait also
places emphasis on the contemplative life which must balance the life of action. Elyot was a firm advocate of classical
learning, and recommended that boys begin such learning
at the age of seven with three authors, Aesop (as a primer),
Lucian, and Homer. Lucian is a relatively obscure author
raised to such prominence only in Elyot. When the William
Byrd of the diary enters the scene in 1709 he will be spending
his mornings contemplatively reading Hebrew and Greek.
From these languages he would read only two authors consistently: Lucian, and Homer.[35] Brathwait is particularly explicit on the value of prayer, as indeed his whole effort is to
Christianize the genre of gentleman's advice literature begun
by Elyot and continued in his own time by Henry Peacham.
In his eventual diary, Byrd was to follow his reflective reading
in Lucian, Homer, and other classical authors with prayer.
Elyot recommends frugality in diet, though not such extreme

frugality as Byrd was to practice when he followed his exercise by eating but one dish at breakfast and indeed at each meal.

Both Brathwait and Elyot go out of their way to recommend dancing as a potentially moral form of exercise despite all prejudices to the contrary. Elyot goes to great lengths to describe a form of dance-as-exercise "now late used in this realm among gentlemen" in whose prescribed motions all the moral virtues might be "founden out and well perceived." He goes on to describe the eight motions of this gentleman's dance and the moral virtues each evokes. All evoke prudence. The first, a bow, also evokes fear, love, and reverence. The second, a motion of the foot, also evokes maturity; the third, providence; the fourth, industry; the fifth, circumspection; the sixth, election; the seventh, experience; and the eighth, modesty. What Elyot describes is a Western version of the Chinese T'ai-chi, which old men still practice with slow grace on Peking's sidewalks early every morning.[36] It is a "dance" with specific physical and spiritual virtues in every single motion. After his prayers and breakfast, the William Byrd of the diary was to "dance his dance" many mornings.

Brathwait then observes that "Privacy is no less perilous than society" and so reminds the reader that the contemplative life must give way to the active. In one of the major sections of his book, on "Acquaintance," he adds that "Acquaintance is a man's security" and is the key to "betterment." Brathwait means these precepts primarily in moral terms, but the implication is left open that acquaintance leads to practical betterments as well. And indeed most English gentlemen of this or any era maintained a wide circle of acquaintances constantly visited in order to "better" themselves. In keeping with Brathwait's emphatic advice and with the actual practices of gentlemen in England, after 1709 the William Byrd of the diary could eventually be seen passing from his contemplative mornings into active afternoons filled with visits and visitors.[37] For Byrd, visiting was to become a mixture of moral conversation, entertainment, status reinforcement, and business, exactly as Brathwait had intended.

Both Brathwait and Elyot recommended above all else moderation, temperance, and self-control. For both, the great enemy is passion. They prescribe examples of how all passions may be controlled. Both recommend a constant review, in Brathwait at the end of the day, of one's success in achieving spiritual control. In Brathwait the control is ultimately a Christian resignation. In his diary, William Byrd was to encode his every emotional response in terms of moderation, balance, and restraint. At the end of each day he was to say, as often as he was possibly able, "Had good health, good thoughts, and good humor, thanks be to God Almighty."

The only thing missing in these vital sources of Byrd's conception of a perfect gentleman as later seen in his secret diary is the diary itself, and this is powerfully implicit in both Elyot and Brathwait. Elyot follows up his opening section on education with a long warning on the "three wayes education maye decaye." Eternal vigilance is needed to keep up a gentleman's learning in later life. Brathwait all but names a diary as the perfect solution to the related problem of self-control, when he speaks of "A Christians Ephemerides; or his Evening account":

> Perfection, at least some small measure or degree therein, is every night to have our *Ephemerides* about with us, examining our selves what we have done that day; how far we have profited, wherein benefited our spiritual knowledge. . . . But principally, are we to looke to our affections which rise and rage in us. . . . O then, let us have an eye to our affections. . . . Let them be fixed then in heaven.[38]

These passages virtually beg a boy embarked on becoming a perfect gentleman through book learning, right behavior, and self-control to keep a diary to monitor his progress.

Finally, young William Byrd's prose style, not later in the laconic diary but rather as he emerged from school in the 1690s and early 1700s, was to be an exact copy of the balanced oppositions and periodic sentences used in Brathwait's concluding portrait of "A Gentleman." Brathwait's specific version of the measured prose of the seventeenth and early eighteenth century, rather than Sir William Temple's or Richard Steele's, was to be borrowed without alteration for Byrd's 1702–1703 portrait of the only model gentleman he was ever well acquainted with, Sir Robert Southwell.[39]

Unlike the works by such other influences as Steele, Allestree, and so on, Elyot and Brathwait do not seem to have been in Byrd's library at his death. But then, neither was William Mason's *La plume volante*, from which he learned the shorthand of the diary. But Elyot's special praise for Lucian and his detailed version of a gentleman's dance as physical and moral exercise are both almost unique to Elyot and, later, to William Byrd. Brathwait's style is unmistakably the model for Byrd's early style. If Byrd did not learn these crucial identifying elements along with others directly from Elyot and Brathwait, then he acquired them indirectly as these authors were absorbed into the curriculum or more generally into the code of behavior at Felsted School or into the several miscellaneous collections and essays on "the gentleman" probably acquired in his school days or shortly thereafter and later found in his library. If these early works were his sources, then not only the conception of becoming a perfect gentleman from books but also highly specific elements of William Byrd's most compulsive personality as it was to be embodied in his diary—with its exact behavioral code and its precise version of the emotional encodement common to early eighteenth-century gentlemen—were very probably complete by the time the boy left school or within a short time thereafter. If so, then the William Byrd of the early 1690s is even in detailed respects the rigid and narrow young man who is to create the texts of the next three decades.

III

As I read him, this younger man Byrd sought nervously for much of his life to equal and to surpass his father's
ambitions for him. These were that he be a genuine Virginia
gentleman, and that he have the equipment to succeed as an
English gentleman, above all through access to imperial
office. Byrd senior tried to get his son a post with the English
Lords of Trade, later reconstituted as the Board of Trade and
the body which administered colonial policy, and he also accepted with equanimity his son's intention, announced at
about this time (1690s) to remain as a lawyer in London, actions which are adequate proof that an English career rising
through the ranks of the imperial bureaucracy to posts just
short of those held by the nobility was acceptable in the father's mind. The younger Byrd's own version of this ambition
came to be a colonial governorship, a post reserved almost
exclusively for English (and Scottish) officers and gentlemen.
If it could be the governorship of Virginia, fine; if not, Maryland would do, but there were longing glances even where the
remote Bermudas rode. Significantly, Byrd's first wife was the
daughter of one of the very, very few American gentlemen to
become governor of a colony. Lucy Parke was the daughter of
Colonel Daniel Parke, erstwhile governor of the Leeward
Islands until his assassination there in 1711. Byrd's very
dreams were obsessively concerned with governorships and
favor in high places in England. His English friendships were
with men well placed to further such ambitions.[40]
    The key word is "nervously." In his quest to fulfill and to
surpass his father's ambition and so to justify his rejection,
Byrd had constantly to expose himself to further rejections
from politicians and from prospective brides and their fathers. He was to receive many, usually pointed at his colonial
status. This exposure renewed for him the rejections of his
youth, and rendered his most vital performances brittle. His
colonial origin and this very brittleness ultimately prevented

him from establishing through marriage or a governorship an unequivocal claim to be an English gentleman and so prevented him from achieving immunity from rejection. What made his performances still less convincing was that his hunger for high marriage and office was also a hunger to be accepted by his own parents-in-the-abstract, and so could bring on painful gushings which bespoke not just flattery but a deep personal need. In the midst of these pursuits, Byrd had constantly to reassure himself as well as the targets of his ambition that he was a gentleman, and he did this by recapitulating obsessively the performances expected of a gentleman. But he did this according to the precepts he had learned at school. Because he had learned the role through written precepts, rather than by absorbing precepts as living metaphors put in practice by a mentor, the performances were rigid and unconvincing at times even to himself.[41] The revenge of such behavior was on his father, and on himself. Byrd was an emotionally handicapped gentleman. It would cost him dearly in the first decades of his adult life.

This behavior can be seen in the texts of his early life, say from 1692 to 1720, and its costs made plain. What should be pointed out first is that in one of these texts William Byrd revealed a similar assessment of his own personality. The most revealing of his early texts is his self-portrait, "Inamorato L'Oiseaux"—the Enamored Bird [plural unintentional]. From internal evidence this seems to have been drafted before the young Byrd returned to Virginia in 1705 though it was re-drafted and sent to a lady friend in 1722/ 1723.[42] It is almost painfully revealing, and is the one great exception to Byrd's tendency to encode himself and to hide himself behind his chosen genre. He speaks first of his laziness and of his mercurial nature. It soon becomes clear that what he is explaining to himself is his failure to succeed in the avenues open to English gentlemen. He confesses his ambition to achieve "the highest pitch of advancement" and recounts his failures. He was "tempted . . . to study the

Law," he observes, "but . . . was soon taken off by the rapine and mercenariness of that Profession." Then "the Gaity of St. James's made him fancy to be a Courteour: but the falsness and treachery, the envy and corruption in fashion there quickly made him abandon that pursuit." When "this fit was over he was charm'd with the Glory of serving in the army, . . . but . . . he was discourag'd by the confinement, dependance, and barbarity of that service." At some moments, "no state appear'd so happy to him as matrimony . . . [but] when he was in love no man ever made so disingageing a figure. Instead of that life and gaity, that freedome and pushing confidence which hits the Ladys, he wou'd look as dismal as if he appear'd before his Judge, and not his mistress. Venus and all the Graces wou'd leave him in the lurch . . . and he was all form and constraint when he shou'd have [had] the most freedome and spirit. He wou'd look like a fool, and talk like a Philosopher, when both his Eys and his Tongue shou'd have sparkled with wit and waggery. . . . No wonder this awkward conduct was without success. . . . Whenever his bashfulness gave him leave to declare his mind something wou'd rise in his throat and intercept the untimely Question. A Woman is with more ease deliver'd of a huge boy, than he was of the painfull secret. His Ey-balls wou'd roul with as much gastliness as if he had been strangled. Twas melancholly to see how his heart panted, his spirits flutter'd, his hands trembled, his knees knockt against one another, and the whole machine was in a deplorable confusion."

Despite its mannered wit, this passage is a perfect description of William Byrd's behavior when caught between his ambition for high office and an influential marriage, and his fear of rejection. Some of his letters to prospective patrons and most of his love letters show precisely this behavior, either "all form and constraint," the book-learned gentleman, or the opposite, a sudden, gushing delivery of his "painfull secret." Byrd also shows some resentment of the rejections he experienced; "he never cou'd flatter any body, no not himself, which were two invincible bars to all preferment. He was much readyer to tell people of their faults, than their fine qualitys." And indeed, a vein of bitter satire against the fashionable London world can be found among Byrd's earliest writings. But generally, while "sorely sensible of Injurys, . . . he punishes himself more by the resentment than he dos the Party by revenge." Perhaps as a result of the dilemma he faced, he became a man who "loves retirement, that while he is acquainted with the world, he may not be a stranger to himself. Too much company distracts his thoughts, and hinders him from digesting his observations into good sence. . . . For this reason he commonly reserv'd the morning to himself, and bestow'd the rest upon his business and his friends."

There were two further features in Byrd's adjustment to his painful experience. One was his initial tendency to blame the rejections he experienced, not on his colonial status (though several were explicitly on this basis) nor on his panic resort to "form and constraint" on occasions of possible rejection, but rather on his "passionate nature." "Love broke out upon him before his Beard, and he cou'd distinguish sexes long before he cou'd the difference betwixt Good and Evil. Tis well he had not a Twin-sister as Osyris had, for without doubt like him he wou'd have had an amourette with her in his mothers belly. . . . This Foible has been an unhappy Clogg to all his Fortunes, and hinder'd him From reaching that Eminence in the World, which his Freinds and his Abilitys might possibly have advanct him to." Passion, even more than his "mercurial nature" or "laziness," seemed to Byrd to explain his failures, and this suggests a deep-seated fear of his own emotional and sexual impulses, often found in personalities haunted by the fear of rejection. This fear of himself would run all through the pages of Byrd's commonplace book, in later life, where the main thoughts and quotations he would jot down would concern control over his emotions.[43] It was perhaps as much to compose his emotions as to digest his thoughts that he spent his mornings alone, and significantly, it was to be on these mornings that he read his books, wrote in his commonplace book, and, probably, wrote in his diary. He presumably emerged from these sessions well composed. For the "Enamored Bird's" final observation about himself is that in spite of all he presented an affable exterior. "His conversation was easy, sensible and inoffensive, never bordering either upon profaness, or indecency. . . . He was incapable of saying a shocking thing . . . and good nature was the constantest of all his virtues." This is true, for, his constipations aside, even today no one can study the man seen in the texts and not like him despite his indiscretions and foolishness. But likability finally shaded over into a studied gentility in Byrd's own self-portrait. Much of the latter part of it is taken up by a lengthy description in highly stylized prose of the "Bird" as a conventional eighteenth-century gentleman. "He knows the World perfectly well, and thinks himself a citizen of it without the distinctions of kindred sect or Country. He has learning without ostentation. By Reading he's acquainted with ages past, and with the present by voyageing and conversation, He knew how to keep company with Rakes without being infected with their Vices, and had the secret of gieving Virtue so good a grace that Wit it self cou'd not make it ridiculous." And so on and on, in a drearily derivative picture of a Byrd all balance, moderation, and acceptance, selling us the universal cultural currency of his age.

A final ambivalence which ran through Byrd's life as a consequence of the forces which shaped his personality can be glimpsed in his self-portrait. This was an inability to decide if he was a colonial or an Englishman. He was unable to identify himself conclusively as one or the other until toward the end of his life. The clear hunger shown in the language of his 1692 enrollment in the Temple, and in his seeking of office and high marriage in England, and even in his pursuit of colonial governorships, was to be an English gentleman. After his initial rejection for the post with the Board of Trade which his father had sought for him, he returned to Virginia in 1696 and was duly elected to the House of Burgesses, but left in haste a year later. The reason for his flight is not clear, as the record is sparse, but from London Byrd told his father that he intended to stay in England as a lawyer. As his own self-portrait suggests, he was not successful at this. When he returned again to Virginia in 1705 after his father's death all the indications are that he did not intend to stay. But he did stay, married, and had children. Reverses then sent him back to England in 1714, where he stayed save for a brief return to Virginia and in spite of further reverses until 1726. In that year he returned to stay but obviously still hoped to go back to England since for years he kept his rooms in London.[44] The dilemma was always that, despite his longing, England never accepted him enough to give him the place or marriage he aspired to, while Virginia never seemed to offer the scope he felt his English education and ambitions deserved. This was an extreme instance of a role confusion experienced by many colonial gentlemen of similar credentials. This confusion did not add to Byrd's credentials a secure sense of place. It adds a touch of poignancy to his observation in "Inamorato L'Oiseaux" that "he knows the World perfectly well, and thinks himself a citizen of it without the distinctions of kindred sect or Country." Put another way, for a long time this enamored Byrd was to find no home. Inamorato L'Oiseaux was this man to a T.

IV

So to the story of this man and his texts. His relationship with Sir Robert Southwell began shortly after Byrd's admission to the bar in 1695. Southwell was a man vastly influential in the colonial bureaucracy, and as such was well placed to help Byrd in the latter's role as agent for his father and for Virginia. Accustomed through his Irish posts to deal-

ing with peripheral gentry, Southwell was well prepared to
understand William Byrd's trepidations in London. Byrd and
his father shared with most aspects of their careers an interest in natural history, and in 1696 in an extraordinary act of
kindness Southwell obtained membership in the Royal Society for twenty-two-year-old William Byrd. He also introduced Byrd to Charles Boyle, who in 1703 became the earl of
Orrery, to Charles Wager, by 1733 first lord of the Admiralty,
and to John Campbell, in 1703 duke of Argyll. If Byrd had
not met John Perceval at school then he certainly met him
through Southwell, and in 1703 Perceval became the first earl
of Egmont. Boyle and Campbell were, like Byrd, aristocrats of
the periphery, the former from Ireland and the latter from
Scotland. These men were to serve occasionally as Byrd's patrons in coming years. In return Byrd made himself useful to
Southwell, most notably in joining Sir John Perceval on his
grand tour of England in 1701. Perhaps inspired by Francis
Bacon's essay "Of Travel," Byrd kept a journal on this trip.[45]
This journal was the first expression of a genre Byrd was later
to adapt to his personality in the form of his diary.

But Byrd's relationship with Southwell sums up the handi-
caps of his personality. His letters to his mentor during the
trip with Perceval are relaxed and calm and there is no doubt
of the very great admiration he felt for Southwell. But when
Southwell died in 1702, Byrd composed a portrait of the man
which is almost unrecognizable. "Cavaliero Sapiente" is almost a parody description of everything an early eighteenth-
century gentleman should be, with no trace of a real human
being known and loved.[46] In studied oppositions and periodic
sentences Byrd enumerates a list of virtues very reminiscent
of his own portrait of himself-as-gentleman toward the end of
"Inamorato L'Oiseaux." "He had the happiness of an early
Virtue in spight of the Ignorance of childhood, and the vanity
and madness of youth. . . . He had alone the secret of gieveing
pleasure to others, at the very moment he felt pain himself.
While he was young, he was wise enough to instruct the old,

and when he came to be old, he was agreable enough to please the young. . . . He had a mighty fond of knowledge, and was always the wiser and better for what he knew. He was so uncorrupt, so untainted with Vice and folly, that who-ever was intimate with him, had the nearest prospect of In-nocence, that he can ever meet with out of Paradise." Three hundred words of this are enough to glaze the reader's eyes. There may be an admission of failure in the fact that in this case Byrd had to add after his Italianate title "Cavaliero Sapiente" the word "Southwell." Without it, not even he would have known who was the subject of the portrait he had drawn.

Byrd's failure here was confirmed by Southwell's nephew, Sir John Perceval. Years later he collected all such sketches of his uncle for a biography. Southwell's daughter Helena LeGrande sent him Byrd's earlier attempt at Southwell. Perceval replied, "I read my unkles character which you sent me with a great deal of pleasure, but think it might have been better drawn: what is said of him is all true, indeed, but I would have it ap-pear like himself all truth without the affectation of wit; it should be composed as by a man that knew him, not one that only admir'd him. . . . I don't mean to find fault with Mr. Byrds sincerity in respect of my unkle, for you and I and all our family know he has a great regard for his memory."[47]

For William Byrd, the sensitive colonial boy ever pursuing the perfect gentleman through his books, it had become im-possible to *know* such a gentleman in reality. Gentility for him was book learning, a set of precepts absorbed from Peacham or from classic seventeenth-century portraits of idealized gentlemen. As a boy Byrd had never had a relation-ship with a significant other, a living model for the gentle-man, to whom precepts were living metaphors to be flexed and transformed by individual experience. By the time he met Southwell it was too late to form such a relationship. Byrd's fear of slights combined with his book-learned sense of his role to send him, as he himself put it, into a frenzy of "form and constraint." He longed for acceptance and admired the man, but could not know him as a unique individual exercising his role as a set of flexible metaphors. He could only see Southwell as he usually saw himself, through a screen of rigid preceptional notions of what a gentleman was. Ultimately, he could not know Southwell as a person. It is a sad spectacle to see William Byrd trying to please this father figure in death and to express his love for him, by throwing at his memory a bundle of preceptual clichés.

One cannot but wonder if Southwell himself had not been aware of Byrd's blocks, and if this does not explain his failure to help Byrd obtain a place with the Lords of Trade. Southwell beyond question had had the power to do this. It may be that he had loved his charming protégé, but known his limitations. Already rejected by William Blathwayt for a position with the Lords of Trade in 1692,[48] Byrd may implicitly have been rejected thereafter by Sir Robert Southwell. Byrd would never know whether his colonial origins or his character were to blame. They were inseparable. Perhaps this haunting possibility had added to the stiffness of Byrd's portrait of Southwell.

Shortly after Southwell died, Byrd became enamored of Lady Betty Cromwell. This was neither the first nor the last time he would aspire to a distant lady far above his position. Lady Betty was by all accounts a witty and much sought-after person, a friend of the playwright William Congreve and the object of many suits of marriage. She had just left for Ireland when Byrd began to write to her in June 1703. Byrd's love letters to her are in a genre he was to become very familiar with through long practice. They are addressed in the style of the age to "Facetia." But in the surviving letters he never succeeds in maintaining the detached and witty tone he aspires to in less serious exercises of this genre. From the very beginning he is, to borrow the words of his own later self-portrait, "laboring" to be "delivered" of his "painfull secret."

Since you went away, I have made a discovery of my self, which I knew nothing of before, that tis not in my constitution to be mad. Were that possible, I'm confident the pain I have felt since you left this place, would have preferr'd me to that condition. Such a choque to my whole nature never happend before; and there is but one thing that can be like it, which is, the parting of soul and body, only this last is more supportable, because it leaves no sad impressions behind it. The moment your coach drove away, Madam, my heart felt as if it had been torn up by the very roots, and the rest of my body, as if it had been torn limb from limb. I coud not have shed a tear, if I might have gaind the universe, or which is better, if I might have gaind you; no, my grief was too fierce, to admit of so vulgar a demonstration. . . . For God's sake Madam have the goodness to write to me very often, and very much. . . .[49]

What is missing here is the gently mocking tone which, in the early eighteenth century, was expected to accompany such hyperbole. Byrd thereby put himself at risk in these revelations.

In a pattern also to be repeated in Byrd's life, Lady Betty does not reply. "For heavens sake therefore," he goes on in his next letter, "be so charitable as to write to me. . . . If you did but comprehend the uneasiness I suffer continually, by not seing you, you woud have more good nature than to add to it, by not letting me hear often from you. . . . To give you some poor instances that I remember you (which God knows I do continually) I have drawn the pictures of 2 of your friends, which I hope will give you some entertainment. In my next I will send you the Widdow Marmousets, and continually study to give you all the diversion I am able. . . . God . . . bring you back full of sympathy for him that is intirely only and for ever yours."

By July, Lady Betty has had enough of her would-be lover's

painful secrets and of his constrained offerings of wit. Once
more in a pattern that is to be repeated in at least one later
case, she writes solely to order him to stop. "No wonder your
Ladyship thought it reasonable to command me to forget
you since you find it so natural in your self to forget your
freinds. . . . Can you believe in your conscience that any body
here values you, loves you and woud do you all imaginable
service and can you at the same time have no sort of value
or remembrance of them?" There follows a brittle, chatty
outpouring of gossip before another lapse, this time into a
relatively stylish melancholy which only half succeeds in
achieving detachment but at least avoids the tedious out-
pourings of his "painfull secret" and the almost hysterical
"form and constraint" of the gossip he offers in hopes of win-
ning her.

Byrd's letters grow longer but Lady Betty does not reply—
"I find Madam to make you speak, is almost as impossible as
to make Babilla silent." Like Babilla, Byrd babbles on, pouring out his heart, offering "the smal entertainment I can give
you" and receiving no reply. Some of his self-revelations are
very painful indeed: "It is the strongest testimony I can give
of my regards to you, to submit my own longing to your tranquility." But to no avail. His only reply an order to stop writing, Byrd dragged the one-sided correspondence on until the
autumn, cloaking his love increasingly in the third person
and disguising himself as "Veramour," then said no more.
One month later, in October 1703, Lady Betty Cromwell
married Byrd's friend Edward Southwell, the son of Sir Robert
Southwell and just beginning his political career in Ireland.[50]

One cannot escape the conclusion from this and similar
cases later, and from Byrd's own self-analysis in "Inamorato
L'Oiseaux," that one part of his ambition was to win not only
the fortune but the heart of a distant lady, a lady distant from
him socially, physically, or in her temperament. Lady Betty
was distant in all three ways. Perhaps Byrd was trying uncon-
sciously to win over the heart of his mother, who, socially

above his father, had agreed to send him and his sisters away and had as far as is known never written to him. He speaks of his rejection by Lady Betty as he might have spoken of his childhood exile, as an expulsion from the Garden of Eden. Certainly, one cannot help wondering if this was not his "painfull secret" when he wrote "For God's sake madam, have the goodness to write to me very often and very much."

The poignancy of Byrd's position in England is perhaps best summed up in the fact that fifteen years later, in the midst of another hopeless suit, he was to call upon two men to serve as his references. One was Sir John Perceval, by then Lord Egmont, who at that very time would be saying so kindly but accurately of William Byrd that he had admired but not really known their mentor, Sir Robert Southwell. The other was Ned Southwell, who had married Byrd's beloved Lady Betty without so much as a message to Byrd, whose subsequent relationship with Byrd was to be distant on his part, and whose family, in Byrd's own words, were eventually to "drop" him completely. Byrd's great charm and persistence kept Perceval as a lifelong if not an intimate friend, but both his recommendors knew of his limitations.

Otherwise the William Byrd of 1692–1705 is the frangible, precious gentleman of his most public self, writing "love" letters and prose portraits with an almost hysterical quality. Some of this tone can be explained by the fact that many of his works were almost surely offerings written for Lady Betty Cromwell in his desperate effort to prove to her that he was an entertaining young gentleman. But these pieces and others also have the air of pieces written by Byrd to prove to himself that he is the young virtuoso of his own dreams. Thus, "To Brillante" and "To Parthenissa" are assemblies of the expected, a sort of wallpaper of clichés to be sent to a lady acquaintance in homage or anger. The same can be said of "Dr. Glysterio," his set-piece portrait of a quack.[51] Byrd cannot seem to build to the surprising and devastating revelations characteristic, for example, of John Dryden's exercises

William Byrd II, probably painted in London before 1705.
See Wayne Craven, Colonial American Portraiture
(Cambridge, 1986), 212–213, for dating of this portrait and
the other portrait of Byrd on page 97, below.
Courtesy of The Colonial Williamsburg Foundation.

in character assassination or of Alexander Pope's later satirical portraits in verse. Instead he papers his subjects with an
even coat of standard witticisms. This general inability to
achieve the sudden revelation either of love or of devastating
insight may account for some of the hysterical tone of these
pieces. Byrd reaches compulsively into his stock of routine
expressions hoping eventually to achieve real wit. What is
characteristic of Byrd as well, is that he would go on writing
pieces like this during his next visit to London, in 1714–
1726.[52] Probably for obvious reasons, London always brought
out the worst in his style.

   In his texts, then, the William Byrd of 1692–1705 is already a hidden man, with no great content beyond obsessive
and mannered clichés. He has few deep friendships, only ambition, and that nervous. Yet he is touching. He is charming.
He is likable. He forms frantic attachments, to political mentors and prospective wives. He writes in an almost hysterical
parody of a late-seventeenth-century gentleman virtuoso's
style. Carousing with the minor literati of the teeming and
diverse London world, assiduously doing his father's bidding
as agent for Virginia with an imperial bureaucracy which has
at least once rejected him, and in general avidly following his
father's advice to get ahead by acting as his father had, by
cultivating patrons and seeking office in spite of all, he is
more transparent than ever he realized. That, probably, is
why people liked him so much.

   V

   So it came to be. In 1705 William Byrd returned to
Virginia to take over his dead father's estate. In spite of his
previously declared intention to settle in London as a lawyer,
he married Lucy Parke and settled in Virginia, living in the
rambling frame house on his father's home plantation at
Westover, near the fall line of the James River. He entered so-

William Byrd's Virginia.
Drawn by Richard J. Stinely.

ciety there in every role expected of him, and more. He sought his father's old seat on the Council and began to seek the governorship itself.[53] In 1709 he emerges into the pages of his diary, the triply encoded William Byrd of historians' frustration. In the context of his personality and previous history he is, however, not so cryptic, he is almost familiar.

It was probably here in Virginia that William Byrd created the secret diary. He had, as noted, kept the journal of his travels with Sir John Perceval in 1701, possibly under the influence of Sir Francis Bacon's essay "Of Travel." Bacon had urged "a young man to put his travel into a little room" by means of a journal, so as to profit from it in self-knowledge and discretion. That would fit our Byrd's character. Bacon had gone on to suggest keeping a journal at home as well, to note "gardens of state . . . comedies, such whereunto the better sort of persons do resort . . . and . . . whatsoever is memorable."[54] Possibly Byrd had extended his travel journal along these lines when he and Perceval returned to London. Similar observations were to be included in his secret diary during his second stay in London in 1717–1721.

A hypothetical early journal could in turn have evolved while Byrd was still in England into something like the secret diaries, as all the main ingredients of the surviving secret diaries were present in Byrd's life before he came to Virginia. An early variant of the shorthand he was to use in the extant diaries was published in 1672. A knowledge of Hebrew, Greek, and Latin, the compulsive pursuit of a gentleman's behaviors, possibly in the specific forms seen in the diary, could all have been products of Byrd's early years in England. We can see Byrd exercising emotional balance, moderation, and restraint in his early letters in pursuit of his father's political ends in the 1690s.[55] An early, Baconesque journal could already have evolved far toward the sort of diaries which survive for the years after 1705.

But if there was an early diary of some sort the odds are that its character changed dramatically once Byrd reached

Virginia. For the diary of 1709–1712 finds him in a radically
new environment in which he practices that genre very nearly
to the exclusion of all others. If the diary is not new to Virginia, then, Byrd's decision to keep it while temporarily cutting off his production of witty letters, portraits, and satires
is new, and this alone must have changed its character.[56]
More importantly, there is persuasive evidence that the secret diary as we know it originated in Virginia after 1705.
The form of shorthand in the surviving diaries is a revised
form first published by William Mason in *La plume volante*
in 1707. If Byrd had learned the older form of Mason's shorthand, from 1672, there would have been little reason for him
to have discarded it in favor of the new, since the old form
was even more obscure and was still nearly as fast as the new.
It is more logical to assume that Byrd first learned shorthand
from *La plume volante* sometime after 1707 and before the
first surviving diary begins in February 1709. This is confirmed by the fact that Byrd seems never to have referred to
ciphers in his letters before 1707, though he does so after,
suggesting very powerfully that he had learned his own cipher
sometime after his return to Virginia in 1705. The secret
diary as such is almost certainly a product of William Byrd's
return to Virginia.[57]

If the opinions of all who have studied William Byrd have
any weight, the secret diary which he created and focused
his attentions upon in this period is the first diary of any sort
(his travel journal aside) that Byrd ever kept. The fact that
Mason's work could not have reached Virginia before 1708,
and that the first surviving diary begins in early 1709 and is
contained complete in one octavo volume suggests that it
may be the very first volume in a new and lifelong creation. If
so, this gives rise to a question. Since his insecurities and aspirations were so intimately reflected in the diary, it was
probably an inevitable device for him to have evolved sooner
or later. The question is why it should have emerged and
come to dominate his production as he began his life in Vir-

ginia. The answer seems to lie in the loneliness and insecurity of a young would-be gentleman in the wilderness.

His father had died in 1704, showing in his will a clear
hope that his son would return to take his place.[58] In spite of
his earlier intentions, Byrd did so. But his father's distant
voice, urging him to improve and sending him specific tasks
as agent of Virginia, was now silent. The will had been his
last message. It was in the winter of 1709–1710, not long
after he began the secret diary, that William Byrd tried one
last time to consult his father, demonstrating in a macabre
fashion his need of continuing guidance from that distant
and symbolic figure. Inevitably he learned that there would
be no guidance.

The winter of 1709–1710 was a hard one. Winter was always the season of death in Virginia, a place where literal
death was more to be feared even than the small deaths of
provincialism.[59] Dreams of death were already haunting Byrd
in a way they never were to do in London.[60] Now, the "distemper" raged in young William Byrd's neighborhood. In December Dr. William Oastler, his friend and physician, had
died of distemper, fever, and drink. Byrd's wife fell persistently ill in what eventually turned into a miscarriage. At
Christmas he took the Sacrament devoutly and early in January dosed his people "to prevent the distemper." By January 8
there were six cases of the distemper on Colonel Edward
Hill's plantation nearby, and the owner himself felt ill. By the
21st four slaves were dead on his brother-in-law John Custis's
plantation and one on his cousin Betty Harrison's next door.
Slaves and masters were dying as the disease moved closer.
Death seemed to be everywhere.

On Sunday, January 22, Byrd rose, read his Greek in the New
Testament, an act unusual for him as he usually read classical
authors, and proceeded to Westover Parish Church. As he was
entering the church, his neighbor Benjamin Harrison's horse
ran away with its coach. The horse and coach careened among
the gravestones in the churchyard, and either its wheels or

the horse's hooves broke down the tombstone over Mary
Horsmanden Byrd's grave. Startled by this evil omen, Byrd returned home to find that his daughter had fallen ill of the
fever. The next night she was so ill that Byrd was disturbed in
his sleep. When Byrd rose on January 24 he was quarrelsome
and could not say his prayers. He went back to the churchyard, nominally to see about erecting a fence to protect his
parents' graves. In this moment of great trouble, he tried to
consult his father. "I had my father's grave opened to see him
but he was so wasted there was not anything to be distinguished." There was no message in his dead father's counte-
nance. William Byrd was alone in Virginia.

Byrd had a strong fence erected around the graves. The
dead doctor's effects were put in order, his daughter recovered, and his wife miscarried. The weather grew warmer
and the sickness waned. William Byrd's father would never
answer the silent question posed that day in the churchyard.
Never close to his son, he was now so wasted that nothing
could be distinguished. But two weeks later Byrd was to note
in his diary, already his most faithful companion and advisor,
that he had amended his creed. Midway in the creed, which is
found in the leaves of the first diary, there is a subtle change
in tone which may identify the amendment Byrd wrote that
day. The creed then continues:

> I believe that Jesus Christ while he livd . . . was [the]
> most perfect Teacher and most perfect Pattern of virtue
> and holiness, . . . that he recommended Righteousness
> by the certain [knowledge?] of Eternal life, and confirmd
> his doctrine of mans [redemption?] in another World by
> his own [resu]rrection.

> I believe that by the [Exposition] of Jesus Christ God is
> [part missing] to accept of [part missing] to obey his
> Laws, [part missing]. . . . That upon his Intercession he
> [part missing] comfort and assist us by his blessed Spirit

to overcome the depravity of our nature and to improve our selves in the ways of Vertue and holiness.

I believe that in Gods appointed time we shall be rais'd from the Dead with bodys purgd from the Dreggs and corruptions of mortality. That God by Jesus Christ will judge all Nations and Generations of men with perfect Righteousness, according [to] the Lights and advantages they had received in this World. That those who have led good and holy lives here will be rewarded with unspeakable happiness hereafter. But those who have obstinately and impenitently Rebelld against God and their own consciences shall go into a State of Sorrow and misery.[61]

It is almost too painful to regard this final part of Byrd's creed, which surely includes the amendment he wrote in that still troubled February, as a reflection also on his relationship with his dead father. But in Christ, Byrd was surely positing a mentor who had been resurrected and who could give him guidance in his time of trouble. The guidance Christ gave, in the name of God the father, was very much the guidance of Byrd's own father in those long ago letters to his son at Felsted School. The message of this "Pattern" was to "improve" in virtue and holiness according to the lights and advantages one had received in this world. If he did not rebel, if he obeyed, William Byrd could expect to be resurrected and rewarded even in a time when death stalked the land. It was the voice of a dead father to a grown boy who now experienced a man's fear of death. It was all William Byrd now had to go on.

This episode may show why William Byrd had already turned for reassurance to his diary. In Virginia Byrd needed advice, he needed reassurance. His father was dead, and the creed only repeated his ancient advice to "improve." Clearly "improvement" was the way to avoid deaths both small and large in this strange environment, but who was to judge an

English gentleman's "improvement" in Virginia? His father
was irretrievably silent, Sir Robert Southwell was likewise
dead, Perceval and Argyll had been left behind. There was not
even a resident English governor in Virginia now that Francis
Nicholson had gone home in a huff and his replacement,
Robert Hunter, had been captured by the French.[62] In all Virginia there was no authoritative voice to remind William
Byrd to meet his father's expectations, to help him to be a
perfect English gentleman, or to reassure him that he was.

After twenty-four years in England William Byrd had heard
often enough that Virginia was a green wilderness. His own
brother-in-law Robert Beverley was even then writing a history of Virginia to convince otherwise educated Englishmen
that Virginians did speak English and that they did not use
their wives as draft horses. Byrd knew better, but he always
felt pressed to demonstrate that a genteel life was possible in
Virginia. Between the lines of his protests in later years, after
he returned there to stay in 1726, one could read real doubt
on his part. Even Williamsburg was just a partially con-
structed capital, and beyond it stretched a largely unsettled
forest. He was then to refer to Virginia as "this silent country" and to observe that moving to "so lonely a country" was
sometimes thought to be like "being buryed alive" and was
"a fair step towards dying." At the time he made these later
observations, he was still keeping his rooms and his books in
London, as an escape should the silence overcome him.[63] The
doubt must have been all the stronger on his first return to
Virginia in 1705.

Should he fill the silence with witty portraits, no one
would listen. No one would ever recognize the Londoners he
satirized and to satirize his fellow Virginians was to risk social death in that tight little world. He tried it only once, in
1710, and was deeply embarrassed to be caught. Love letters
as a genre were out, since they were taken seriously, not as
flirtations, and any woman in Virginia would be likely to accept Byrd in a flash. How was William Byrd to know he was a

gentleman? By early Virginia's ambiguous standards he was, but he had always aspired higher than this, and in 1706 married the daughter of the only Virginian ever to achieve status as a colonial governor. How was he to know, however, in the silences of Virginia, that he was an English gentleman, until he himself, as he now repeatedly sought to do, achieved that unquestioned status as the king's governor? [64]

The diary was the answer. In it William Byrd the gentleman found a mirror which was at once a form of reassurance and a record of mastery. In the absence of other voices, above all his father's, once distant and now silent, William Byrd desperately needed to be sure he was still a proper gentleman by the standards which he had set for himself. He needed to know that he was still on the road to which his childhood aspirations, born in pain, had pointed him. The diary served this function. He turned compulsively, obsessively to it as to a counselor, or as to a mirror. In the silence of having outlived his mentors and left the only true society for a gentleman, William Byrd needed his diary. Curiously, Byrd did not seem to maintain much contact with his most elegant friends in England by letter. Much later in life, on his second return to Virginia in 1726, Byrd would seek counsel and reassurance by letter from his old acquaintances in England. For some reason, perhaps because after Southwell's death all the others were as young as he, he did not do so now, on his first return to Virginia. He began the diary instead.

So the boy's project of becoming a perfect gentleman went a step forward, and in Virginia became a secret diary. This became the only genre of his first adult years in Virginia and the dominant genre of his life. The diary became a mirror in which a man in his thirties still unsure of his emotions and status, and far from the social mirrors of London, could review his vital performances. He was never to let go of it.

The diary was in a shorthand code for reasons familiar from Byrd's character. There were in Virginia no places "whereunto the better sort of persons do resort." There was

little that was "memorable" in the meaning of Sir Francis
Bacon.[65] A tentative gentleman would be a bit ashamed to
pursue a journal in such a place. But the nakedness of his
need for the diary was probably the main reason for Byrd's en-
cipherment of that instrument. Byrd needed the reassurances
the diary gave him that he was still in all respects what his
father had seemed to send him away to be, a perfect Christian
gentleman. But no gentleman wanted it to be known that he
needed to look at himself in the mirror of his diary every day
to check his pose, as it were, and to reassure himself. A fellow planter stumbling on an English diary in Byrd's mode
would have thought him precious or vain. A discoverer might
have seen the insecurity beneath and so known Byrd in his
deepest secret.

Since the rejections of his childhood, which had been
reinforced by later rejections by officials and prospective
brides, Byrd had been sensitive and withdrawn. His mornings
were always spent alone, "ordering" himself, as he so often
put it. His commonplace book as well as his diary was to reflect a concern with controlling his emotions.[66] To be seen to
be so insecure that he had constantly to review his own performances, would have been an agony of revelation for Byrd.
Though such was not the main stuff of the diary, to have his
sexual feelings and political ambitions known would have
been no less painful. In Mason's shorthand, no such revelation was likely. To make certain, Byrd not only hid Mason's
book but also put locks on the doors of his library where we
may assume the diary was kept.[67] As will be seen in a set of
love letters written after the death of his first wife, Lucy, Byrd
was one day to cast his deepest emotions in cipher in still
another genre. He would make them known in plain English
only once in his life.[68] The irony, of course, is that in general
Byrd's behaviors and emotions were so encoded in his diary
that little was overtly revealed in comparison with the secrecy in which it was kept.

The shorthand code may have been intended above all to

hide Byrd's further-encoded self from his wife. The book
from which he learned shorthand was published shortly after
his marriage, and the first surviving diary begins less than
three years after the marriage. Rejection by women and an attempt to control his sexual emotions run all through Byrd's
life from his youth on. Shortly after the diary begins, in April
1709, he is furious with his wife for listening to him from
the top of the stairs. On another occasion he was to refuse
her a book from his library. His control of his emotions, recorded in the diary, was to concern above all control of his
emotions with respect to his wife.[69] It may be that above all
else Byrd did not want Lucy to know him. He could not toler-
ate this intimate a relationship with a woman. His marriage
may have helped send him to his diary for privacy, and it
probably led him all the more to keep his diary private. Fortunately William Byrd was transparent enough for Lucy to
have known him anyway and Lucy was not a woman to be
ignored, so the marriage, even as seen in the pages of the secret diary, was passionate in spite of the bounds of secrecy
Byrd placed on himself.[70]

The behavioral code which Byrd now came to review in his
secret diary was the final distillation of his project to be a
perfect gentleman. The origins of this code lay in his school
years, and in Peacham and Allestree, but it was probably built
up further in the early 1690s with the help of Steele and
Temple. Its deepest sources plainly lay in Elyot and Brathwait. Because the behavioral code was learned largely from
reading and casual observation rather than from a close relationship with a mentor, it was probably a bit stiff from the
beginning. There is no early diary, so we cannot prove that
Byrd practiced such a code daily before coming to Virginia or
with what flexibility. But in the stiff compulsiveness of his
use of conventional gentleman's genre in this early period,
and in the relentless clichés of his portraits of himself and
Southwell as gentlemen, we can see some previous versions
of the rigid ideal which William Byrd was now to review

daily in his secret diary. Up at five, read Hebrew and Greek, pray, exercise, do accounts, read Latin, eat lunch, do business and visit, read more Latin, see slaves and wife, pray, and have good health, good thoughts, and good humor thanks be to God Almighty.[71] The shock of Virginia seems to have turned a stiff view of the gentleman's role into an unvarying daily routine which had compulsively to be reviewed in secrecy. At a minimum it certainly required that such behavior be compulsively reviewed in secrecy. It also meant that such a review in the diary came to dominate Byrd's written production.

The behavior seen in the diary is profoundly preceptual. The actions carried out seldom vary. They are usually practiced in perfect order.[72] They are always expressed in the same language in the diary. The actions, their order, and the language in which they are described express a precise, narrow, unvarying conception of a set of highly specific events which have very nearly a ritual significance. The daily review of these events seems also to be a part of the ritual. A gentleman reads in the ancient languages (Elyot, Temple): "Read in Hebrew and some Greek in Lucian." A gentleman exercises (Elyot, Brathwait, Peacham): "danced my dance." A gentleman prays (Brathwait, Allestree): "said my prayers." A gentleman contemplates and then actively pursues acquaintance (Brathwait): "Ate milk for dinner. Visited Colonel Harrison whence we went to Falls Creek." A gentleman is composed with Christian heroism (Brathwait, Steele): "had good health, good thoughts and good humor thanks be to God Almighty." Virtually never does Byrd as he reviews himself in his diary transform the ritual language he gave these book-learned precepts or break out to apply them as living metaphors implying more subtle qualities of a gentleman's place within his culture. He does not comment on the virtues of Petronius versus those of Cassius. He does not enthuse about sport. He does not reflect on the content or efficacy of prayer or on the virtues of reason versus faith, as a living gentleman would be bound to do. Perhaps Byrd did such things in real life, though from all indications seldom, but in his diary he is reviewing a litany of actions-seen-as-the-fulfillment-of-those-precepts-which-a-boy-once-learned-would-make-him-a-gentleman. It is a rigid, almost unbending set of poses aimed at his father's ambitions for him. This litany, in his constant secret review of it, defines his relationship to his culture. It defines William Byrd as a handicapped gentleman, reviewing as precept what he often proved unable to practice as metaphor. This is what he now reviews in his so secret diary. It is to this code that he now turns for reassurance.

Perhaps the most important thing to remember about Byrd's behavioral ritual, however, is how much it was performed alone. This admittedly sensitive man who "loved retirement" was alone in his locked library from five or six in the morning sometimes until noon, and again in the afternoon or evening, reading in languages, "dancing," praying, writing letters and accounts. He was also alone when at some point he reviewed all this in his diary. Half his waking hours were spent in the solitary performance and review of a shy colonial-turned-gentleman.[73] It is as if he lived eternally in his youth, each day becoming a gentleman in large part alone and from books and, equally alone, examining his progress in the diary. This prolonged solitary routine was the basis of his ability then to go out and pursue "acquaintance" in society. Without it, he could never have managed his public life. When he did go out into society, as will be seen, he would eventually pursue his most crucial ambitions with the same clumsy rashness which had already typified him as a suitor. The common theme was a fear in the face of possible rejection which would by his own admission mar his life. So the Byrd of the diary, and in life, was a profoundly shy and solitary man before he was a glittering social being.

The emotional encodement also practiced in the diary is less unusual in its form. It is the classic stance of any eighteenth-century gentleman in control of himself. Byrd had already practiced this in his early official letters. All that is unusual in the diary is his new compulsion to record his mastery of his emotions and then to review his overall success daily as part of his behavioral ritual: "had good health, good thoughts, and good humor thanks be to God Almighty." Self-doubt had always lent an edge to Byrd's need to control his feelings, and in the diary and in his commonplace book he found the means to be sure that all was emotionally in order as he moved toward fulfilling his ambitions in Virginia.

In the privacy of his mornings alone, then, in the privacy of his library, in the privacy of a shorthand diary, William Byrd daily reviewed his ritual of precepts fulfilled and recorded his mastery of his feelings. He was ready for whatever Virginia might offer.

The diary is both cryptic and expressive. What it expresses is the history of William Byrd's personality as it encountered Virginia. Old elements of the sad schoolboy trying to be a perfect gentleman coalesced into the three codes of the secret diary, in a form of Byrd's personality which would remain essentially unchanged. Flashes of the old London virtuoso with all his painful longings leaking at the seams would recur on Byrd's disastrous return to London in 1714. But even then he kept up the diary. Eventually the virtuoso would be replaced by the essayist, and the diarist would slowly mature into a man somewhat less compulsively bound. But for all his life the personality and its genres were to be dominated by the triple codes of a diary through which William Byrd sought reassurance and mastery over himself as he arrived in Virginia. In some sense this would be the final form of his personality. Byrd's life became the diary, and the diary was to express his life.

V I

Compulsive in its secrecy and in its regularity, obsessive in the set pattern of each day, which disturbed him when it was disturbed and was disturbed usually only when he was most disturbed, the diary became a continual written mirror in which Byrd could see himself and see that he was indeed a proper gentleman in style and in substance. The result above all of his childhood exile, of his later compensations for this, and of his arrival in Virginia, his daily primping is a sad and a brittle, an unwilling revelation. Yet the diary cannot be seen simply as the fulfillment of a personality created by childhood trauma. The relationship between Byrd's personality, diary, and life was far richer than this. For one thing, just as William Byrd was always more alive and more likable than his earlier use of genre would indicate, so the William Byrd of the early diary was always more alive and likable than his encoded self in the diary. His diary permitted him this much self-expression. Moreover, he seems initially to have found both reassurance and mastery by means of the diary. All of this can be seen in the diary, and to understand it is to understand in its most subtle dimensions what the diary captures as well as to understand why William Byrd was so successful in his early Virginia career.

In the spaces between the items in Byrd's behavioral ritual, the tone of moderation, balance, and restraint which he sometimes also raised to an object of obsessive observation nonetheless also functioned successfully for him as it did for many eighteenth-century gentlemen. This tone could be obsessive when, for example, he felt obliged to reassure himself at the end of a perfectly ordinary day, as a part of his ritual, that he had "had good health, good thoughts, and good humor thanks be to God Almighty." But at other times, before he got to this formula or even by means of it, he could use the code of emotional restraint in a way which was entirely in keeping with its more normal uses by his contemporaries. One clear function of such social and emotional politesse was to create a universally acceptable social personality, rather like an international social currency, by which differences might be minimized and by which all persons with credentials of any sort known in an appropriate way. The jarring reality of differences, differences in personality, background, ideology, religion, ambition, and in fortune, was to be ironed out by a smooth gentility proud of its acceptance of all who conformed to its easing rules. Three, no, four things were anathema to this cultural system: class differences rudely expressed, or violated, by all who were not gentle; to be disturbed by vicissitude; to show a fatally desperate ambition; and to show (usually religious) enthusiasm. One could avoid these pitfalls, all perhaps linked to the violence of the preceding century but still anathema because of its persistence in the eighteenth century, and in the process could avoid questioning the honorable intentions of others similarly engaged, by assiduous attention to the easy graces of a social, linguistic, and emotional style which, in Byrd, often differed little from that style as embodied in other gentlemen.[74] It served him as it served them, to place him as a citizen of a cultural world in which he belonged.

Thus, when he recorded that he had "kept his composure" during one of Lucy's tantrums, he was maintaining emotional credentials which identified him as a successful and not a pathological gentleman. When he regretted his sexual pecadilloes, as on November 2, 1709, when he records kissing another man's wife "which I should not have done, because I ought to beg pardon for the lust I had for another man's wife," he was again reaffirming a code which made him a gentleman neighbor and so preserved social harmony. When he reprimanded the master of the grammar school at the College of William and Mary for being drunk, as he did on June 7, 1709, he was not being a religious prude but was reminding a man with genteel pretensions that gentlemen might be "merry" but never "drunk."[75] This, too, was a way to guarantee a common standard of social behavior within which eighteenth-century gentlemen could deal with one another. Byrd naturally strove to meet that standard himself. Much of his reading in Tillotson and Allestree was an effort to remind him of such goals.

Equanimity was the key to a uniform social behavior free of unreliable extremes and unreconcilable differences. Such equanimity had to be kept on the most trying occasions, or it would have meant nothing. It sometimes seemed callous, as when Byrd's infant son died on June 3, 1710. "We went out and found him just ready to die and he died about 8 o'clock in the morning. God gives and God takes away; blessed be the name of God." But such composure in the midst of pain was the stuff of a cultural order hammered out with great labor following the chaotic Puritan Revolution of the previous century, a cultural order which permitted the aristocracy to maintain successful control not only of its emotions but also of Anglo-American society throughout the eighteenth century.

The political uses of this emotional code could be seen in an event which happened only three weeks after Byrd's son died. The man to whom he had lost the governorship of Virginia, Sir Alexander Spotswood, had just arrived in Williamsburg. Despite his grief, Byrd rode in to attend his rival, expecting at least to be continued as successor to his father on the Council. But the governor's instructions made no mention of Byrd, and he was seated only after a protest from other councillors. There seemed no end to Byrd's disappointments. Despite disappointment and sour wine, he struggled to maintain the behavior expected of him.

We went to dinner at Court where the President [of the Council] treated us. . . . In the afternoon we retired to the President's to drink the Queen's health, where I drank some French wine that did not agree with me but gave me the gripes. In the evening we returned to Green Springs with the Governor but I could not enjoy him because of my indisposition. However he always distinguished me with his courtesy. I took leave of the Governor this night, because I resolved to go early in the morning. I neglected to say my prayers but had good health, good thoughts, and good humor, thank God Almighty.[76]

A bereaved father, a doubly discouraged politician, and a man with a sour stomach, William Byrd played out the courtesies of this ceremonial day and managed to record good health, good thoughts, and good humor when it ended. His Christian stoicism had made him a good companion in spite of all, and the governor had done his part by repaying his courtesy in full measure. Behind the seemingly obsessive formula that evening lay a true gentleman.

This emotional style, this way of being—it went that deep—could be profoundly expressive. Modern observers, used to a post-romantic culture in which feeling may be and usually is expressed explicitly, cannot understand the way in which, in eighteenth-century culture, feelings were expressed by their restraint. It was so in eighteenth-century Japan, and in Sweden and Germany. In Japan and Sweden, it still is today. In such cultures one need say very little, and subtle variations in conventional politenesses express volumes of agony, sadness, joy, love. No one misses these signals and their powerful emotional content will be discussed exhaustively among intimate friends in private. Sometimes the silences between the conventional words and the very tone of those words are enough to convey the power of the emotions straining against these conventions. So it was with the conventions of William Byrd's day. No man needed this fact more than the otherwise constipated William Byrd. Here was an eloquence which his nature could accept and his culture approve.

The very day Byrd was disappointed in being omitted as a councillor in the governor's instructions is a case in point. After the initial confusion over his credentials, he attended all the day's ceremonies. Only a sour stomach, a failure to enjoy the governor, and a polite but early departure, all of which even to himself he blamed on the wine, showed his upset. He implicitly admitted the true source of these troubles was his disappointment by confessing in his diary that by the time he retired he had "good health." Though in his continuing chagrin he neglected to say his prayers, he managed also in the end to achieve "good thoughts and good humor." Very little of his feelings had peeped out between the conventions as he dined and traveled in state with the others or even later as he wrote in his diary. Only one familiar with the diary and with William Byrd's psychosomatic illnesses could see in his recovered health by evening that his heart and not his stomach had been hurt. Only one familiar could know that his neglect to pray was for him a characteristic symptom of psychic upset. But Alexander Spotswood knew, and saw, and always on that long day distinguished William Byrd with his courtesies. Small hidden messages of psychic upset were treated very seriously in this silently eloquent age. It was a mercy for a secretive William Byrd and yet it also establishes how expressive he was in the fashion of his age. One had always in this age to listen to the silences between the words.

Byrd's restrained expressiveness in the diary went far beyond his reaction to minor political contretemps. He was eloquent in the face of death itself. When his son had died, earlier that same June, Byrd had been "griped" in his belly, as he was to be purportedly by sour wine but really by political disappointment three weeks later. After the formulaic "God gives and God takes away; blessed be the name of God" he records that neighbors came immediately "to see us in our affliction." Characteristically, as he was to do all his life, he then projected his feelings onto his wife. "My wife was much afflicted but I submitted to His judgment better, notwithstanding I was very sensible of my loss, but God's will be done." "Very sensible of my loss" spoke volumes of agony for an eighteenth-century sensibility. We do not hear, as they did, the long pauses between the words and the pain in every word. "My poor wife and I" were to go walking, "my wife" was to cry and need consolation, for days to come. As for Byrd, his stomach griped him, he had indifferent health, he neglected to say his prayers as he struggled visibly to stay "within the bounds of submission." Not even after June 6, when the child was buried while the Byrds watched from the church porch in a driving rainstorm, could Byrd return to his evening formula in his usual, peculiar testimony to the composure which his time required of him.[77] No one present at Westover in those days could have missed his grief.

The same could be said years later, when his wife died in London. Byrd then conveyed his grief in a moving if brief letter to John Custis. "Gracious God what pains did she take to make a voyage hither to seek a grave. No stranger ever met with more respect in a strange country than she had done here, from many persons of distinction, who all pronounced her an honor to Virginia. Alas! how proud was I of her, and how severely am I punished for it. But I can dwell no longer on so afflicting a subject, much less can I think of anything else, therefore, I can only recommend myself to your pity, and am as much as any one can be, dear brother, your most affectionate and humble servant, W. Byrd."[78] In the push of emotion against the restraints of convention, in the attribution of respect for her to others, in speaking of his concomitant pride instead of his love for her, and in refusing to dwell on her death, while admitting that he could not "think of anything else," William Byrd was grieving for his wife in the irretrievable eloquence of another century.

Before Lucy died, there was to be much joy. The joy was entered cryptically in the diary, in short sentences. "Quarreled with my wife," "walked with my wife in the garden," "we were very merry." But once one is used to filling in the silent spaces between these sentences, as between the conventions of restraint, and once one sees how thickly such notes fell on the pages of the diary in 1709–1712, there can

be no doubt that William Byrd was a loving man. In these no-
tations he was no more cryptic than many a bluff country
squire. The diary is full of quarrels and reconciliations, intimate walks in the garden—an activity usually reserved for
Byrd and his wife alone—passionate worries about his sick
daughters, romps with visitors, and bored, rainy days together. One day he quarreled with his wife and by afternoon
was giving her a "flourish." "It is to be observed," he notes,
"that the flourish was performed on the billiard table." On a
rainy day at a friend's home, the Byrds and other bored guests
waited for the rain to let up. When it did, they went outside
and began to play a children's game called "burning coals."
In the lavender afternoon dark, these fine adults could have
been seen romping gaily.[79] Save that he wrote in shorthand, in
such entries Byrd's diary was not cryptic. It was expressive.
He simply did not, like Pepys, associate the mere number
of words with expressiveness. The early eighteenth century
may have used, and needed, few words to express its joys.

The diary shows that Byrd was capable of genuine friendship as well, and here too, his feelings frequently attained expression in spite of the laconic nature of his diary. Amid all
the small business consultations and the compulsive visiting
with which the Virginia, like the English, gentry passed their
time and reinforced their social contacts, many friendships
emerge. As the diary begins, Dr. William Oastler is already a
close companion, as is the Reverend Mr. Charles Anderson,
rector of Westover Parish. In one sense the too convivial physician and the sturdy parson were stock figures straight out
of any country gentleman's retinue. But Byrd clearly cared
for both men, for their "merry" times together with other
friends, for their discussions, card games, and travels together. When each passed from his life, Byrd looked after his
dead friend's affairs. He never found an adequate replacement
for either.[80] Similarly, Byrd's neighbor, Benjamin Harrison of
Berkeley, was if not a close friend certainly a constant one in
the first years of the diary. The two families were frequently

together and were, like most Virginia families, cousins by
marriage. During Harrison's last illness in April 1710, Byrd
and Lucy were foremost among the friends constantly at
Berkeley plantation to keep watch with the dying man. At
Westover Byrd sent frequently for news of Harrison, sent
small delicacies to tempt his appetite, and recorded repeatedly that all were "melancholy" at this time. The final scene
was recorded with care, something most unusual in the diary.

> Mr. Harrison . . . died . . . this morning, which com-
> pleted the 18th day of his sickness, according to Mrs. Bur-
> well's dream exactly. Just before his death he was sen-
> sible and desired Mrs. L— with importunity to open the
> door because he wanted to go out and could not go till
> the door was open and as soon as the door was opened he
> died. The country has lost a very useful man and [one]
> who was both an advantage and an ornament to it, and I
> have lost a good neighbor, but God's will be done.[81]

The Byrds comforted the widow, and after the funeral, William
Byrd of all people reacted angrily to the "extravagant panegyric" by which the minister hid the faults as well as the real
virtues of his neighbor.[82]

Byrd's closest friend for many years was to be his brother-
in-law John Custis. Custis had married Lucy Parke's even
more tempestuous sister Frances on the same day that Byrd
had married Lucy in 1706. In their letters he and Byrd were to
commiserate over their extravagant and willful (as they saw
it) wives and over the tangles of their father-in-law Daniel
Parke's estate until long after 1714, when Byrd had left Virginia for his second stay in London. Their letters also ex-
changed confidences on their common struggle against Alexander Spotswood. Custis's expertise as a tobacco planter was
probably a source of great help to his novice brother-in-law.
The friendship faded after 1718 partly because of recrimina-
tions over the handling of the Parke estate but largely because after his wife's death in 1715 Custis moved back to the

Eastern Shore and so was out of reach when Byrd returned from London in 1726. But for the years from 1706, when each married, until 1718, when the friendship began to fade, William Byrd and John Custis were best friends.[83] Byrd stood as godfather for Custis's only child, Daniel, on October 28, 1710, and five years later it was to Custis that Byrd confided his feelings when Lucy died. Something of this easy ongoing relationship with "brother Custis" can be seen in the diary, but by and large its simple calm references to the man are a good example of the almost totally unspoken expressiveness of this instrument.

In its slow evolution a final friendship, seen exclusively in the diary, seems to have expressed beautifully the accommodation with his own feelings which William Byrd was achieving in these years and achieving partly through his diary, where these feelings were in fact recognized. When, on June 22, 1710, Byrd's great rival Sir Alexander Spotswood had arrived to assume the governorship of Virginia, he had brought with him his provocative mistress Mrs. Katherine Russell and, to Byrd's evident surprise, his physican, "my old school-fellow" Dr. William Cocke. As Byrd showed the governor's gentlemen attendants around his plantation in July, it soon became clear that it was Dr. Cocke's approval that mattered most to him. All others faded from view. What mattered was that Dr. Cocke "seemed to be well pleased with the place." Byrd showed him his library with which Dr. Cocke, "a man of learning," was "pleased" as well. Later that day, Byrd noted that "Dr. Cocke and I played at piquet and I won." Throughout most of 1711 Byrd tried determinedly to turn his old schoolfellow into a replacement for his previous retainer, Dr. Oastler, by repeatedly forcing payment for medical assistance upon him. Cocke tried to render this help out of mere friendship, but Byrd pressed money upon him. He used Cocke to distribute his tips to Spotswood's servants. He teased him unmercifully until he became angry. "We" of the Council, Byrd noted in April of 1711, "did not choose Dr.

Cocke" for the board of the College of William and Mary, because he was "not an inhabitant."[84]

Byrd's nervous attempts to impress and then to subjugate
his old schoolfellow suggest once again that he had felt
slighted as a colonial boy at Felsted. Plainly he was going to
display his superiority in Virginia to Dr. Cocke at every opportunity. This behavior was inappropriate, as Cocke was
Spotswood's confidante as well as his personal physician.
Byrd had increasingly to go through Cocke to reach Spotswood
or to read the governor's intentions.[85] By 1712 Spotswood's
trust was to make Cocke secretary of state of Virginia, an
office which would place him on a par with the members of
the Council. But throughout 1711 Byrd, in spite of his own
interests and in spite of the good doctor's patience in serving
Byrd both medically and politically, continued energetically
to patronize his old acquaintance. He criticized him for in-
terrupting him, criticized him as dull, and tried once again to
impress him, this time with his sawmill.[86]

But Cocke's great patience achieved a gradual revolution in
his relationship with William Byrd. He willingly treated
Byrd's friends and effected at least one notable cure. The
turning point came in July of 1711 when Byrd himself fell
desperately ill with malaria. Cocke nursed him through a
violent delirium lasting a week. Dr. Cocke "came . . . out of
pure friendship and not as a doctor. . . . The Doctor told me
he would stay with me till I was safe, notwithstanding he neglected a great deal of other business . . . [and that] this distemper made me very [unclean] and burdensome. . . . The
Doctor saw me in a good way and so took his leave but he
took nothing for all his trouble, which amazed me. . . . I gave
him a million of thanks since he would take nothing else."
Two weeks later Byrd assured a friend that Cocke would treat
the friend's brother, who had come down with smallpox, the
most dreaded contagious disease of the early eighteenth century.[87] If he actually did this, Cocke was risking his life to
confirm his friendship with Byrd.

After these episodes Byrd slowly came around. Suddenly he called Cocke "merry" and by Christmas observed, "the Doctor was very pleasant company, as he commonly is." Later still, "we were very merry as we always are with the Doctor." Byrd came to lean exclusively on Cocke for medical care. More and more, as he and Spotswood came at loggerheads, he depended on Cocke for political advice and for access to the proud governor. Byrd tried feebly once more to make a joke at Cocke's expense, and again to pay him, but these behaviors eventually disappeared. By early 1712 the doctor and his wife were close friends with Byrd and Lucy, and the doctor was his family as well as political confidante. Cocke's growing political power was shown in an incident in which, in the midst of helping Byrd in his struggle with the governor, *the doctor* sent *his* coach for Byrd! By the time Cocke's commission as secretary of state came through, Byrd put up Cocke's security for the latter's performance in the office and seemed to share Cocke's resentment of the governor's "double-dealing" with regard to Cocke's commission.[88] In Byrd's biased eyes, at least, the new "Mr. Secretary" was now his stout bulwark against a governor whom neither could trust.

Byrd had Cocke to thank for their new friendship amidst sickness and political strife, but he responded to the man with a warmth which the diary does not hide. Byrd's own ability to overcome the jealousies of his school days in order to accept William Cocke as a friend, and his willingness to record this friendship in his diary, were both testimonies to his increasing acceptance of his own feelings in these Virginia years. The diary literally served as the instrument by which Byrd admitted to himself that he felt this friendship. In recording the friendship, both he and the diary were outgrowing their origins in the shocked compulsiveness of a schoolboy turned perfect gentleman, all at sea in Virginia.

One theme ran so pervasively through William Byrd's life and first diary from its first pages to its last, that it emerges in retrospect as one possible vehicle of Byrd's tentative evolution from compulsion to confidence in these years. That theme is death. In retrospect it is inescapable that death was the central fact of life in Virginia which William Byrd had to overcome if he was to survive there as a sane gentleman. The question Byrd had faced on coming to Virginia had not simply been how he could survive as an English gentleman there. It was how he could survive at all, and mentally, in an environment still so ridden with disease and death. This was the pointed version of his eternal query "what shall I do" which he had put to his dead father in the graveyard in the deadly winter of 1710. It was to this question that Byrd sought an answer in Christ, the incorruptible, and in God the father, as he went on to write his creed. A year after he had reburied his father and written his creed, in December of 1710, death was again to strike alarm into William Byrd in the most haunting of a series of dreams of death which marked his first years in Virginia. This time there was to be no doubt of the awesome dimensions death assumed in the mind of the young gentleman with his new family and responsibilities. Death was again abroad at Westover as he wrote:

Some night this month I dreamed that I saw a flaming sword in the sky and called some company to see it but before they could come it was disappeared, and about a week after my wife and I were walking and we discovered in the clouds a shining cloud exactly in the shape of a dart and seemed to be over my plantation but it soon disappeared likewise. Both these appearances seemed to foretell some misfortune to me which afterwards came to pass in the death of several of my negroes after a very unusual manner. My wife about two months since dreamed she saw an angel in the shape of a big woman who told her the time was altered and the seasons were changed and that several calamities would follow that confusion. God avert his judgment from this poor country.[89]

The compulsiveness of Byrd's early diary could be read in part as a need to hold off the fear of death, of literal bodily dissolution as well as of dissolution as a proper gentleman, by consulting a rigid code of behavior and by maintaining emotional balance in the face of the imminence of death. That this was so could be seen in Byrd's most rigid rule of all, apparently made early on in Virginia, to eat but one dish at a meal. The diary begins on February 6, 1709, with this rule in full form: "I ate chocolate for breakfast. . . . February 7, 1709. . . . I ate milk for breakfast. . . . I ate nothing but beef for dinner." On February 11, 1709, "[the Harrisons] stayed to dinner, when I transgressed the rule." This latter instance is the only time Byrd actually speaks of a rule in his life and uses the word *transgressed,* a strong term for him. In this dietary ritual, as in his almost equally compulsive dosings of his slaves, his family, and himself, we may see a literal set of rituals against the pervading death of Virginia. The diary incorporated these behaviors in a larger set of figurative rituals aimed against death as well as against cultural dissolution.

The measure of the expressiveness of this diary in spite of all its compulsiveness is its ability to show, even by its restraint, love in the face of death. William Byrd's most hard-won friendship, that most warmly expressed in his diary, was that with Dr. William Cocke, who in his view had saved him from death. The diary, perhaps, was a holding action against the shock of death until, in the face of death, in the face of Virginia's winters of distemper and fever and summers of malaria, life could assert itself. Life did assert itself, at first emerging between the formulae of the diary and finally in the friendship with Dr. Cocke, warming into an assurance of survival until it overcame even childhood prejudices.

Yet at the same time literal death was still only a version of the figurative death William Byrd had always faced, the death of not justifying the pain of his childhood and indeed adult rejections by becoming a perfect gentleman.[90] And the reassurance seen in the diary as it progresses through 1709, 1710, and 1711 was also a reassurance against this fear. The key to this reassurance lay in a fourth code, really a theme, which ran through the diary of these years. In this theme one sees William Byrd's insecurities being far more powerfully assuaged than by his achieving emotional expression in the face of death. This theme is mastery. For beneath the paraphernalia of secrecy, beneath the behavioral rituals and the most compulsive of the emotional encodements, and beyond the restrained and hard-won expressiveness of this diary, the larger theme which emerged was Byrd's mastery of the new roles of the Virginia gentleman-extraordinary. In vignettes stashed away between the machineries of the diary he watched himself trying out the roles left him by his father. In hundreds of little dramas he acted out and reviewed his performances as family man, plantation owner, militia leader, and politician. In his successful mastery of these roles he found reassurance. He also found delight. Obnoxious as it is at moments, this delight pervades the pages of the diary until once again we cannot help but share his joy.

Mastery over his wife could not have been easy. Lucy Parke Byrd was not as wild as her sister Frances, but she was clearly a trouble to her husband. Controlling her was more than a matter of controlling his emotions, it was a daily struggle for the upper hand. She objected in no uncertain terms to Byrd's public flirtation with married women, she criticized his manners and his business deals, and she even took his authority on herself and reprimanded a guest for swearing. Sometimes Byrd's control over her was arbitrary, as when he made her sell off her silks because he was worried by temporary business reverses, or when he refused to let her pluck her eyebrows before a ball at the governor's palace. But at other times she was plainly willful and violent.[91] On July 15,

1710, "My wife against my will caused little Jenny [a maid] to be burned with a hot iron, for which I quarreled with her." Six months later: "My wife quarreled with me about not sending for Mrs. Dunn when it rained. . . . She threatened to kill herself but had more discretion."[92] Mrs. Dunn, the wife of a parson who subsequently abandoned her, was eventually taken into the Byrd household at Lucy's request. A troublesome guest, she made life hell for Byrd by posing further challenges to his authority and by tyrannizing the servants. In Lucy's most towering scene of all, on March 2, 1712:

> I had a terrible quarrel with my wife concerning Jenny that I took away from her when she was beating her with the tongs. She lifted up her hands to strike me but forbore to do it. She gave me abundance of bad words and endeavored to strangle herself, but I believe in jest only. However after acting a mad woman a long time she was passive again.

In rescuing his authority Byrd was often literally concerned with rescuing the servants.

Similar trials would cause John Custis to rejoice once Frances Parke Custis had died in 1715, and to note in his epitaph that his brief years of bachelorhood before he married in 1706 had been the only happy years in his life.[93] Byrd showed a much more tolerant view of Lucy. Despite frequent quarrels and a constant, tense awareness that he must uphold his "authority," Byrd soon learned that authority was best maintained through reconciliation. "My wife was out of humor this evening for nothing, which I bore very well and was willing to be reconciled." Next day: "In the evening my wife and I took a walk about the plantation and were good friends. . . . I gave my wife a flourish."[94] True, in Byrd's eyes "rogering" his wife or giving her a "flourish" was a form of reconciliation which smacked of a self-satisfied mastery achieved through sexual aggression. But more gentle forms of reconciliation and so of mastery were also common. The

night after the worst scene of all, when Lucy had beaten
Jenny with the tongs and then tried to strangle herself, "we
drank some cider by way of reconciliation and I read nothing."[95] Here as elsewhere, Byrd's routine could be discarded
when reconciliation was at stake.

Possibly Byrd found the patience to bear Lucy because he
knew she needed patience to bear him and his craving for authority. Possibly he was tolerant because she was usually ill
when pregnant, was pregnant most of the time, and miscarried easily and often. Whatever its source, it was at times a
gentle patience Byrd exercised and a mastery as often distinguished by companionship as by arrogance. The calmest of
the calm things William Byrd did in these years was to walk
so many evenings with his wife alone in their garden. The
witty evenings with friends, the day he and his wife took a
nap and had a "roger," held nothing as calm as these walks.[96]

Mastering his "family," as Byrd referred to his five or six
house slaves and several dozen other slaves on the home
plantation at Westover, brought out all the ambiguities of a
humane man indulging in slavery. Lucy's violent determina-
tion to work her will on the house servants shocked Byrd repeatedly into defending them. His objection was always to
the violation of his authority as master and to the irrational
passion and severity with which Lucy inflicted punishments
rather than to the idea of corporal punishment itself. Yet at
times even more measured forms of corporal punishment
were a reality he preferred to keep at a distance. The third
entry in the diary, for February 8, 1709, records that "Jenny
and Eugene [house servants] were whipped." Though on occasion he "had" slaves whipped, Byrd preferred the impersonal "were whipped."[97] Whipping was something his overseers did and he could pretend simply happened. This of
course evaded the turbulent realities of his household, in
which slaves frequently fell victims to his or more likely to
Lucy's ire, but it did mean that for Byrd mastery was not always to be found in the direct act of whipping a slave or even

in the act of ordering a whipping. As often, he found it in being the center of a system of authority in which slaves "were whipped." His own involvement in acts of mastery over his slaves was limited to smaller cruelties. "Eugene pissed abed again for which I made him drink a pint of piss."[98] Time would erode even these perverse satisfactions, and by the time of his final diary in 1739–1741 William Byrd would have achieved a radically different relationship with his slaves. In the meantime, mastery over his slaves was shown in a more positive if somewhat rigid manner. Whenever death threatened "his family" or "his people," Byrd went out to the quarters to treat them. The "dosing" or "vomit" he gave them was an impersonal action in a medical role which masters were expected to fill, but it entailed risks of contagion nonetheless. Moreover, it is clear in context that "my people" were more than an investment to be saved. They were an extension of Byrd himself and as such were to be protected from death.[99] In protecting them, he asserted his mastery in yet another act reviewed with confidence in his diary.

Mastery brought reassurance in other areas of plantation life, often in a rather studied fashion but with delight as well. Every page of the diary contains entries such as these on its first pages: "Daniel [Wilkinson, an overseer] came from Falling Creek where all things were well and the sloop almost loaded"; "I sent a boat and two hands to Appomattox for the pork"; "The people made an end of tarring the house."[100] Byrd is quite unlike another Virginia diarist, Landon Carter, in that he never in these entries or in his letters shows a systematic sense of detailed planning toward the overall management of his plantations. There are no accounts of yields and profits, schemes for improvement, or comments on their implementation, as in Carter.[101] Byrd did ride out to survey his distant plantations twice a year, but on these occasions as well the entries read simply "I went to the Falls where I did not find things in so good order as I expected. . . . I gave the necessary orders, and after dinner went in the rain to Appomattox, where I found all things well."[102] Rather, what appears to have mattered to Byrd in making these entries was to be *seen* receiving Daniel Wilkinson's report, to be *seen* ordering the boat to Appomattox, to be *seen* having his people tar the house. Likewise on his round of his plantations, what mattered was to be seen judging affairs at the Falls, to be seen giving the necessary orders, and to be seen riding on to comment with approval on things at Appomattox. Byrd needed to be seen, by himself, doing these things. In such cases the diary became a mirror which permitted William Byrd to review his performances as a planter. He reviewed them as they arose rather than as part of a ritual. It is evident that he found them good.

Retainers and neighbors danced the dance of society around the Byrds, and the diary was a record of these triumphs as well. Dr. Oastler and Parson Anderson, Robin Mumford and John Banister, physician and parson, client and apprentice, whirled around William Byrd in accompaniment to his centrality at Westover. In his diary he touched on their subsidiary performances as attendant lords to swell his scene. Neighbors came constantly to visit. They came in such numbers after church on Sundays that the Byrds' servants could not go to church themselves for all the preparing they had to do. Eventually Byrd would have the church moved to solve this problem. The vestry, on which he served, had confirmed his social rank by giving him "the best pew in the church," so he could hardly be surprised that he was the social sun of parish society.[103] The diary records the events testifying to this status with quiet satisfaction.

Byrd was at his most delighted and most vain, however, in recording his political progress. First it was the vestry, where he was the star. Then, in April of 1710, he was made the commander-in-chief of the Henrico and Charles City county militias. "I was appointed commander in chief of two counties"[104] may sound cryptic, but it is one in a long series of cryptic satisfactions in the pages of the early diary. As militia

commander Byrd presided every year at general musters of
the two counties' militias, which were massive ceremonial
occasions richly recounted in the diary. Often the governor
would ride out but always Byrd was the man of the day, with
attendant officers meeting him to do homage en route to the
muster. Once there, a stern review of the ragged militia was
followed by sports, prizes, speeches, and punch. In one case,
"I caused the troops to be exercised by each captain and they
performed but indifferently for which I reproved them. One
of the French [Huguenots] was drunk and rude to his captain,
for which I broke his head in two places." Whereafter, "I
caused the men to be drawn into a square to see the men play
at cudgels." Next day he stood as judge in the militia court,
cautioned some Quakers that he would fine them if they did
not serve, and dismissed the men.[105] Byrd's performance as
commander was never indifferent, nor was he indifferent to
its glories. The height of his delight came when he led his
men in the midst of an actual war scare in 1711. Amidst
alarums and excursions over the sighting of what was feared
to be a French invasion fleet, Byrd recorded himself acting
coolly to dispose of his men to meet any threat. In the midst
of his unspoken joy he kept a sharp eye out for the presentation he was making and for the better one he might make:
"Major [Wynne] had his holsters at his girdle and an armor
bearer that carried his pistols, which made a good figure."[106]

The vestry and militia were mere preludes to higher office.
One such office Byrd had arranged to inherit from his father
and had had confirmed to him before he left England, the
post of receiver of His Majesty's revenues in Virginia. It was
worth hundreds of pounds to him but it was a diminished
post, as his father's accompanying place as auditor of those
same revenues had been taken from his son at his death. So
Byrd made little of his role as receiver-only in his diary save
to note that he strove to get the receivership and auditorship
rejoined in his hands as they had been joined in his father's.
He concentrated instead on the next of his father's posts, that

of member of the Council of State for Virginia. This in turn
was to be a jumping-off point for a higher place than his father had ever held, the governorship of Virginia or, as a second choice, of Maryland. By 1708 Byrd had heard from England that he was to be appointed to the Council. He was
sworn in on September 12, 1709, "God grant I may distinguish myself with honor and good conscience." He then began to write to friends in England for help in, and to dream
of, being made a colonial governor.[107] This is the stage he had
reached as the first diary was begun early in 1709. It in turn
records his further successes, and some failures, as he reached
for ever higher rungs on the ladder of his political ambition.

His local triumphs at home at Westover, in his parish, and
in the militia seem to have created a confidence which initially carried over into Byrd's struggle for higher office as seen
in the diary. Many things should have eroded that confidence
by the middle of 1710. In a stunning rejection, the duke of
Marlborough had replied to his suit for the governorship to
the effect that "no one but soldiers should have the government of a plantation."[108] This effectively ruled out colonials.
Byrd's infant son had died, and the new governor, Alexander
Spotswood, had arrived without mention of Byrd's position
on the Council in his binding instructions from the king. All
this is recorded in the diary, which also shows that this con-
juncture of rejections (the latter of which was soon rectified)
daunted Byrd only briefly. He continued to dream of favor
from England, and he plainly enjoyed every moment save the
first of the new governor's progress through the colony. When
Byrd entertained Spotswood and his retinue at Westover or
performed before Spotswood as militia commander every detail of the governor's response was recorded. Echoing a very
similar comment by his father years before, Byrd observed
that the governor "showed me great respect." Spotswood had
gone out of his way to compliment and to reassure his erstwhile rival and William Byrd had enjoyed the flattery.[109]

The confidence of mastery gave this diary its final tone of

assurance and even joy. Byrd was alive, not dead, and he was also in his own view a successful husband, master, neighbor, Virginia aristocrat, and potentially an imperial politician. The satisfactions involved were deep. William Byrd had entered into almost every role and place occupied by his father. He was receiver general and seeking to have the auditorship restored. He was a member of the Council and so ex officio a judge of Virginia's highest court. He had, as his father had not had, high connections in England whom he could still hope would raise him to a governorship. Whatever his father had wanted of him, surely he had succeeded at a part of it now, in so successfully filling his father's place in Virginia. This is what he saw in the mirror of his diary. Byrd's unspoken joy was the joy of conformity to the will of his dead father, then, but it was also the surprised delight of a man who had at last found an environment in which he could triumph. Virginia may have been empty and frightening in some respects, but he had begun to master it. Byrd is never more touching than in his success. He had come into his own and, for the moment caught in his diary, was on his way to realizing his dreams.

VII

William Byrd seemed to be escaping from the worst compulsiveness of his own project to become a perfect gentleman. In Virginia he had faced the twin threats of literal death in this mortal environment and of the figurative death of provincial life, which would have destroyed his project. He had incorporated his need to survive and to continue improving into a fundamentally compulsive diary. But he was a young man and he had survived death itself, and so life had leaked out around the edges of his compulsions into love and friendship. Most of all, his inherited status had seemed to guarantee him mastery over the social and political environment of Virginia, and in this mastery he had found a content-

ment visible in the diary. Inner needs based so clearly on his
father's needs for him as he read these, had come into conformity with his new environment through a rapidly successful
performance as his father's heir. What his father had done
in forty years he had done in five. The problem was that a
harmony based on such external success was vulnerable. As
soon as his further ambitions met real resistance in the external environment, William Byrd was to shatter. His personality was to prove more permanent than circumstance and it
would soon come back to haunt him.

Yet the collapse was more than just the product of external
circumstance. Byrd brought on himself the events which
were to return his personality to a more compulsive state
than ever. To read right up to and beyond the boundaries of
the first diary in 1712, is to sense that there was a pathology
at work here which would shortly cost William Byrd the life
of his wife Lucy and ten years purgatory in London. If this
were a Greek tragedy, it could be said that like any tragic hero
he overreached himself. For in 1711 and 1712 Byrd reached
for his ultimate ambition, a colonial governorship, in two
ways, one symbolic and one actual, both of which brought
his house down around him. But in terms of his previous history these actions were not so much a tragic overreaching as
an inevitable pursuit to the bitter end of his father's ambitions for him as he had long interpreted these. In Byrd's mind
the aim had always been, manifestly from his texts, to become an English gentleman. In Virginia this had become the
obsessive pursuit of a colonial governorship, the only way in
which a colonial gentleman could establish beyond doubt his
status as an English gentleman. After 1711 he was to pursue
these versions of his childhood need nearly to personal and
political destruction. If evidence were needed that Byrd's personality was in some sense pathological, the years from 1711
to 1720 would provide it. In the process, Byrd and his writings became the macabre skeletons of a compulsive personality without redeeming flesh.

The origins as well as the result of these events can be seen in the diary. The first of Byrd's deadly actions was a deceptively simple one. On December 7, Daniel Parke was assassinated by a mob outraged at his performance as governor of the Leeward Islands. Parke's will left everything to his daughter Frances Parke Custis on condition that she and John Custis pay his outstanding debts. Lucy received nothing but the thousand pounds long ago promised as her marriage portion. Byrd's reaction was that his wife had been "fobbed off" with a trivial inheritance which might not ever be paid out of the estate in the Custises' hands. Parke "gave me nothing but gave his estate in this country to my sister Custis" as Byrd put it in his diary.[110]

This may have been one rejection too many for Byrd. In 1710 he had failed in attempts to obtain the governorship of Virginia and that of Maryland. The duke of Marlborough's gruff "no one but soldiers should have the government of a plantation" had doomed a colonial's hopes for either position to the realm of dreams. Byrd had continued to dream, of course, with the mixture of fear and blind hope ever characteristic of his desperate ambition: "I dreamed last night that the lightning almost put out one of my eyes, that I won a tun full of money and might win more if I had ventured, that I was great with my Lord Marlborough." But by the time the Parke will was proved late in 1711 all dreams of success had disappeared. By January 1712, they had given way entirely to dreams of death. This time, the dreams of death were unprecedentedly personal and immediate: "I dreamed a coffin was brought into my house and thrown into the hall." Three days later, on January 19, 1712, "I dreamed a mourning coach drove into my garden and stopped at the house door." Death and the death of his ambitions for himself had been powerfully associated in his creed, amended after he had exhumed his father two years earlier, and they may well have been associated now.[111]

In any event, suddenly on February 2, 1712, "we went to

Colonel Duke's and by the way my brother Custis and I made a bargain that I should have [Parke's] land and negroes that were [otherwise] to be sold by act of Assembly [to pay Parke's debts], and pay all Colonel Parke's debts." This startling move displeased Lucy, perhaps because she knew all too well her father's spendthrift ways.[112] She may have sensed the possibility of a hidden mountain of debt, something Byrd never considered in his haste. But she finally consented and the deal was done. It is inescapable that Byrd's developing ambition to become governor of a plantation had found symbolic satisfaction in his marriage to Daniel Parke's daughter. Now, six years after his marriage and just as his ambitions seemed to be unreachable and death alone ruled his dreams, he rashly assumed the dead Daniel Parke's "estate"—literally in the meaning of the eighteenth century assuming Parke's status in Virginia. He refused to let John Custis and the Virginia Assembly sell off what he plainly viewed as "his" inheritance.[113] He took full responsibility for Parke's assets in return for relieving his brother-in-law of the debts. But Lucy and Custis had been right, and Byrd hasty, for the legacy of Daniel Parke was nearly to crush him.

Late in 1711 Byrd also began to take a more aggressive line in his relationship with his great rival, Sir Alexander Spotswood. This was to be his second fatal step. Spotswood, the soldier who became governor instead of Byrd, had begun to show a strict sense of what the king required of his lieutenant in Virginia. By this time it was becoming clear that Spotswood wanted reform of the revenues, of the tobacco economy, and of the judiciary in ways conducive to the king's income and power. He was beginning to view the magnates of the Council of State as a set of intermarried allies determined to thwart him in this effort to execute "the King's will" and he later called the Burgesses a "mean" lot.[114] Such blunt diplomacy gave Byrd's suppressed ambitions an opening he could not resist. As soon as he scented resistance on the Council and in the Burgesses to Spotswood's latest request for special funds to be placed at the governor's disposal, Byrd wisecracked that "no Governor ought to be trusted with £20,000." The indiscretion quickly became known and the governor angry.[115] By their next meeting, on January 24, 1712, the governor "made us wait half an hour before he was pleased to come out to us and when he came he looked very stiff and cold on me but did not explain himself." Byrd may already have used his wit at the expense of Spotswood's mistress, Mrs. Katherine Russell,[116] and now he had offended the governor irretrievably.

From this point on, Spotswood lost no opportunity to cut Byrd. His "courtesy" disappeared from the pages of the diary to be replaced by a strictly businesslike relationship as the early diary ends in 1712. In 1713, instead of helping Byrd reunite his father's offices of receiver and auditor-general of the royal revenues, Spotswood began to challenge Byrd's administration of the receivership. By late 1713 this had become a running battle in which Spotswood was pointing out to the Board of Trade in London that a Virginian such as Byrd could not be trusted with thousands of pounds of the king's money![117] It looked as if Spotswood's revenge would be completed by Byrd's removal from the receivership. A victory for Spotswood would have deprived Byrd of his father's old office and cost him hundreds of pounds in vital income, income all the more vital as Parke's debts were by now proving larger than Byrd had thought.

So, late in 1713, William Byrd sought permission to journey to England.[118] His primary reason was to discover, if he could, the limits of the ever-growing lists of debts which Parke had left behind and which Byrd must now pay. But in time it became evident that Byrd had also gone to England in pursuit of his battle with Spotswood. His aim was at least to protect his receivership, and possibly to add the auditorship to it, thereby restoring all his father's offices to his own hands. Rumor had it that he also went to try to unseat Spotswood and to take his place as governor of Virginia.[119] As with

the Parke debts, Byrd had bitten off far more than he could
chew. The other members of the ruling faction on the Council were willing to use Byrd as their occasional agent in their
escalating disputes with Spotswood. They may also have
found the foolishly ambitious Byrd a useful stalking-horse
with which to test the wind in Whitehall, in case Spotswood
was weaker there than they feared. But events proved that the
councillors were not yet ready to try to remove Spotswood in
a head-on battle. Some of them would have been horrified by
the thought of Byrd as governor. As Nathaniel Harrison later
put it to Philip Ludwell, leader of Byrd's faction in the Council, "consider the consequences if Col. Byrd should ever obtain his [end] and come here governor and we should be so
unfortunate as to differ with him. That Col. Byrd will come
here in that stature I have [now] much reason to think and
therefore we should act so as not to give him any advantages
against us."[120] Fortunately for his political associates, the
rumor proved untrue. But clearly the Council was not allied
with William Byrd in all his ends. As for support from the
Burgesses, Byrd had done little to cultivate them. In November 1710, he had insulted them with a "lampoon" which he
had thrown over a wall into the capitol in Williamsburg. By
1713, then, his envious tongue had offended the Burgesses,
the governor's mistress, and the governor himself, and his
ambitions had frightened at least some of his fellow members
of the Council. With this dubious support he went to England to challenge Spotswood, who had powerful friends in
the colonial administration. It was a battle in which Byrd
would have some surprising successes, but which he was
doomed to lose. It would nearly cost him his political career.

Byrd arrived in London by July 1714.[121] The scale
of the double disaster he had brought on himself took time
to unfold. It could be glimpsed in Byrd's letters home to
John Custis even before its full dimensions emerged in the
pages of the second of the surviving diaries from 1717 to

1721. The Parke debt grew steadily throughout the more than ten years, 1714–1719, 1721–1726, Byrd was to stay in London struggling to escape the consequences of his hasty ambitions. By 1726, perhaps £3,000 in debts had surfaced which Byrd had had no knowledge of in February 1712 when he took on the estate. This was equivalent to two years' income from all of Byrd's sources.[122] He blamed Parke and his agents, Perry and Lane, for not giving him complete information earlier.[123] But it was Byrd's ambition which had persuaded him to buy this pig in a poke. He was to spend the rest of his life paying these debts, until they haunted his waking hours and at times his dreams, and he was to remain in debt to Perry and Lane, who had loaned him the money to pay Parke's creditors, nearly until the day of his death. His own version of his father's horror of debt seems to have hounded him more than the debt itself, which by his old age in the 1740s was down to £1,000, not excessive by later Virginia standards.[124] In an ambition shaped to please his father, he had reached for Parke's estate only to fall into a debt which would have shocked the old man.

Debt was the growing background to the main drama played out in London, Byrd's effort to justify himself, and to challenge Spotswood, politically. In pursuing his ends, Byrd was to have some initial successes. He was despite his rashness slowly to weave together all the threads of opposition to the governor and so to become one of the central figures in a vastly larger political event; namely, Virginians' more general resistance to their governor. This resistance, in turn, would become a landmark in the colonists' efforts to gain greater control over their own affairs.

Spotswood had been clever at first, in not revealing the full dimensions of his desire to reform every aspect of the colony's administration. In his initial years in the colony, from 1710 to 1712, he had cultivated the magnates of the Council. He had moved cautiously to try to persuade the Board of Trade, England's primary agency for supervising the colonies, to add

to the Council's appointive members men such as Dr. William
Cocke, whom he hoped would be loyal to his purposes. In a
similar fashion Spotswood had sought to manage the House
of Burgesses to make its membership more amenable to
his wishes.[125]

But by 1714, when Byrd had left for London to defend his
own handling of the receiver's position, the governor was
hard put to conceal his impatience with the entire spectrum
of Virginia politicians he faced. In seeking to reform the col-
lection of the king's revenues by improving the methods practiced by the receiver general and by the auditor, Spotswood
had provoked a confrontation with an intermarried set of
large planters who controlled most of the twelve seats on the
Council. He had further offended this faction by attempting,
as early as December 1712, to carry out a provision written
into his instructions from the crown, to create a new high
court of oyer and terminer in the colony. This court would
have rivaled the Council itself as the high court of Virginia,
and Spotswood made it clear that he intended to break the
Council's monopoly of supreme judicial power by appointing
men to the bench who were not on the Council. While the
resulting opposition by members of the Council proved more
cautious than Byrd had expected, his hopes of their support
while in London were not to prove entirely in vain.

In 1713, shortly before Byrd had left for England, Spotswood had disturbed another sleeping bear in the form of the
House of Burgesses. Spotswood's Tobacco Act, put before the
Burgesses in that year, was a sensible enough proposal. By
providing official warehouses for storing and evaluating tobacco, it would have created, in the form of receipts for a
given quantity and quality of tobacco stored, a reliable currency for use within the colony, and would have helped raise
the standard of tobacco sent to England by preventing the ex-
port of the very worst grades. Expending every ounce of political credit he had left, and manipulating votes by offering
every office and favor he could dispose of, Spotswood suc-

ceeded in getting the Tobacco Act through both the Council and the House of Burgesses. But he purchased his victory at too high a price. Alarmed by the expense of the warehousing system and by Spotswood's manipulation of votes, Virginia's voters rose against the governor. The next set of burgesses, elected later in 1714 and sitting in 1715, voted to repeal the act. Still unsure of whether to win over or to oppose Spotswood, the Council helped the governor by voting to block the Burgesses' repeal of his favorite act. From this point on, the House of Burgesses, which had over the past fifty years evolved into an institution ever more sensitive to its constituents' concerns, was to be constantly in opposition to the governor. Because of the Council's caution and continuing narrow concentration on its own interests, the House of Burgesses was to lead the opposition to Spotswood.

In London, William Byrd was to be ideally situated to harvest this growing discontent to his own ends. Beginning in 1715 he was to assist the Burgesses by seeking to persuade the Board of Trade to veto the Tobacco Act. At the same time, he would successfully couple opposition to the Tobacco Act with opposition to Spotswood's Act for the Better Regulation of the Indian Trade (1714), which threatened Byrd's own interests in that trade. By 1717 the Burgesses were to appoint Byrd their official agent, in London, with repeal of both acts as their goal, though neither Spotswood nor the Board of Trade was ever to acknowledge the Burgesses' right unilaterally to employ such an agent. At about this time, in October 1716, Spotswood once again tried to appoint to the court of oyer and terminer some of his political allies who were not members of the Council. The result of this provocation would be that by 1717 Byrd was to become at last the acknowledged agent for the majority faction on the Council as well, in their tardy but determined decision to fight the energetic governor. Byrd would thereby gather all the reins of discontent into his own hands. His greatest successes were to come in mid-1717, when the Board of Trade was to repeal both the Tobacco Act and the Indian Trade Act. In the process, the members of the Board were to urge Spotswood to be more cautious in pursuing his other schemes, such as that to appoint noncouncillors to the court of oyer and terminer.

But Byrd was to purchase these interim victories only by inviting the progressive destruction of his political reputation in London, and by creating a continuing suspicion of his ultimate ambitions on the part of his fellow councillors. For one thing, the Burgesses' opposition to Spotswood was never quite respectable in the eyes of the authorities in London, who had a low opinion of the rights and membership of representative bodies in the colonies. Byrd was never fully to be recognized as the official political agent for this "mean" lot, as Spotswood had described them. Also, the Council, as noted, was to be slow in coming out against Byrd's great enemy. When the majority of the Council did emerge into open opposition, they, like Byrd, would pursue their narrow ends, in this case the destruction of the court of oyer and terminer, so obsessively that they would first ignore and later nearly undermine in their self-preoccupation a promising alliance with the House of Burgesses. The unsavory spectacle of an "implacable" William Byrd, mustering such (respectively) "low" and selfish opponents to the governor while pursuing his own legislative and personal ambitions, would play nicely into Alexander Spotswood's hands. From the beginning Byrd had constantly to defend himself, and always ran the risk of losing everything he had achieved politically if Spotswood could prevail upon his many supporters on the Board of Trade to remove Byrd from all his offices on the grounds that he was a troublemaker. In the end, by 1719, Byrd would face exactly that devastating prospect, and would be sent home in disgrace to make his peace with Alexander Spotswood.

In the early years of his stay in London, then, 1714 and 1715, Byrd had just begun to learn the magnitude of the Parke debts. Politically, he possessed only indirect support from the Burgesses and cautious encouragement from some of the Council as he began waiting on the colonial bureaucrats in London. He called sometimes with his own petitions defending his conduct of the receivership and sometimes with complaints about other items from Spotswood's range of reform legislation. When in 1716 Spotswood complained himself that Byrd could not remain receiver general of His Majesty's revenues in Virginia while living in London (and while trying to thwart His Majesty's governor, he might have added), Byrd sold the office for £500 and used the money to finance his campaign.[126] In effect he cannibalized his father's old office to reach for still higher things. At this point, Byrd was as yet only a presumed agent for some members of the Council and implicitly for the Burgesses. But, as members of the Council well knew and as some of them feared, he was now using these presumed statuses to unseat his main rival and so to claim the governorship for himself.[127] Byrd was to pursue this aim obsessively in the face of all discouragement for the next three years. He persisted even when Spotswood petitioned the crown to have the Board of Trade remove Byrd from the Council. The slow growth of opposition to Spotswood in Virginia was enough to keep Byrd's ambition alive. So were the Virginians' minor victories against their enemy.[128] But throughout, it was Byrd's own ambitions he pursued in the face of mounting evidence that Spotswood was too strong to be removed. He had staked everything on this ambitious course and he could not let it go.

By 1716 Lucy was tired of waiting for her husband to return home, so she made him a visit on her own in the autumn. They toured the countryside together, and he introduced her to London society. But in December she died of smallpox in London.

She was taken with an insupportable pain in her head. The doctor soon discovered her ailment to be the smallpox, and we thought it best to tell her the danger. She

received the news without the least fright, and was persuaded she would live until the day she died, which happened in 12 hours from the time she was taken. Gracious God what pains did she take to make a voyage
hither to seek a grave.[129]

Byrd's agonized letter on her death hides the further agony he
must have felt knowing that his own foolish ambitions had
caused Lucy's death. But within two months he had found a
third quest which would keep him in London even beyond
the empty pursuit of his two other mistakes, and which
would prove equally fruitless. He was out to find a rich wife.
It is this William Byrd who steps before the mirror of the second diary on December 13, 1717, one year exactly after he
had written John Custis of Lucy's death.[130] He is a driven man
running from imminent failure.

For its first years, 1717–1719, this diary is a product of
growing debt, of deepening political frustration, of the death
of his wife, and of Byrd's failure to find a rich heiress to take
her place. By 1718 it is more and more clear from his correspondence that Spotswood's friends in England have the
power to remove Byrd from the Council and so to deny him
the last of his father's major offices.[131] Byrd's desperation only
increases apace. The product of this desperation, the diary of
1717–1719 is scarcely bearable to talk about. The tone of
tense sterility which has blocked so many scholars is simply
the product of years of accelerating failure. The diary is the
record of the failure of a personality as well. The buoyant life
of the young man in Virginia has drained away. So has the joy
in mastering a new environment. What is left is Byrd's empty
pursuit of misplaced ambitions gone wrong on the scene of
his own previous failures. London society had not given him
office or a rich wife before. It would not do so now, for now he
was an aging failure of forty-three, still pursuing ambitions
painfully above his station. This knowledge only intensifies
his searching. The result, in terms of the diary, is that all one
sees is the hollow routines of a nervous boy now combined

with those of an aging roué. He turns compulsively to the skeletal behavioral routine established in the Virginia diary, but now he fleshes it out with restless visits to the theater, to whores,[132] and to prominent gentlemen in whose social mirrors he hopes to shine (and who are sometimes not at home to him).

26. [January 1719]. I rose about 8 o'clock, having taken my asses' milk, and read a chapter in Hebrew and some Greek in Lucian. I said my prayers and had milk porridge for breakfast. About 10 o'clock came Annie Wilkinson and I rogered her. About one o'clock I went to Will's and read the news and then went to Mr. U-t-n to dinner and ate some boiled beef. After dinner we went and sat with U-m-s and drank tea and about 5 o'clock I went to Will's where I sat the whole evening till 9 o'clock and then went to Court where were abundance of pretty women, and Mrs. F-r-m-t-n among the rest with whom I talked abundantly, and then said many things to Mrs. B-r-n. Here I stayed till eleven and then went home in a chair and said my prayers.

27. I rose about 8 o'clock, having had my asses' milk, and read a chapter in Hebrew and some Greek in Lucian. I said my prayers and had milk porridge for breakfast. The wind was west and it rained. Captain [Blakiston] came to borrow a habit for the masquerade and I lent him one. About eleven I went to visit my daughter and offered a ticket to Miss Page but she would not accept. Then I went to Mr. Lindsay's where I dined and ate some roast veal. I gave Mrs. Lindsay a ticket. After dinner we sat and talked, Miss [Coatsworth] being there. About four I went to Garraway's Coffeehouse and from thence to Mrs. Cole the milliner. Then I came home and Annie Wilkinson came and stayed till seven. I got ready my dress which was a gray domino and a red head. About eight Mr. Lindsay and Mr. Jackson came to my lodgings

and I carried Mr. Jackson to Lady Guise's and from thence
we went to the masquerade where I was not much di-
verted but stayed till 6 o'clock and then came home,
much tired, in a chair and neglected my prayers.

28.   I rose about 11 o'clock, having had my asses' milk,
and read a chapter in Hebrew and some Greek in Homer.
I said my prayers, and had milk porridge for breakfast. I
danced my dance. About one o'clock my Lord Percival
came and stayed about half an hour. I read some English
till 3 o'clock and then ate some brains. After dinner I put
several things in order till 5 o'clock and then I went to
see Mrs. U-m-s where I drank tea and stayed till six and
then went to Will's, where I met my Lord Orrery and
went with him to Mrs. Smith a [g-t] woman that lives in
Queen Street where I met with Mrs. C-r-t-n-y and went
to bed with her and rogered her two times. We lay till 10
o'clock and then rose and I went to Will's and ate a jelly
and then walked home and said Lord have mercy on me.

He no longer had "good health, good thoughts, and good
humor thanks be to God Almighty"; sometimes he could
scarcely utter a desperate prayer.

Surely such a life could not have gone on for long, yet the
diary gives the impression that Byrd could have gone on for-
ever in this restless unsatisfying round in search of he knew
not what. The answer may lie in his growing failure to find
the end of the Parke debts, to unseat Spotswood, or to find a
rich wife. It is as if Byrd could not return to Virginia until he
had had some success. His letters to John Custis give the
same impression.[133] So he went on searching, searching for a
success which would send him home with honor or for one
which would keep him in London as a rich husband. It was
an older, more desperate man, perhaps aware of his own
foolishness, who now wandered the streets of London, and
the pages of his diary, looking for a way out. He was a parody
of his youthful self.

By this time the denouement of Byrd's stay in London had already begun with a catastrophically failed romance. Early in 1717 Byrd began to notice outside the window of his rooms in the Strand a pretty young lady leaving and entering the Beaufort Buildings across the way. His inquiries revealed that she was Mary Smith, younger daughter of John Smith, the wealthy commissioner of the excise. Someday she would be rich. Byrd began his suit with a compulsive secrecy typical of the man but which also revealed his own sense of vulnerability. He was after all an aging colonial and a political leader seeking the hand of a London heiress in her early twenties. He first contrived to meet her at a masquerade ball where his face could not be seen. He then instructed her by letter in the use of a "cypher" of invisible ink. By June he was pouring out his love to her in letters secretly sent from "Veramour" to "Sabina" in this cipher. Pathetically, the cipher failed to reveal anything, as "Sabina" tartly noted in a letter which nonetheless led Byrd on.

TO VERAMOUR.

July 1, 1717.

I receiv'd the letter you sent under the Name of Madam Turnover, and had reason to beleive there was more in the Paper, than was expresst in Black and White. Before that, I had two Billets from you under the like discreet Disguize, and did not doubt but this brought a third of the same tender kind. I therefore went to work in all hast with my Decyphering Elixir, in order to extract your meaning, and bring all that Tenderness to light which I imagin'd you had wrap't in darkness: but to my great Surprize and disappointment, I cou'd not make one syllable of it appear. How much this baulkt my Curiosity, I ought not to tell you; all my Comfort is, that you kindly intended to write me something about your Passion: but made use of so feeble a sort of Liquid, that it cou'd by no means express it. I give you this freindly notice, that you may take more care another time, and not give me the pain of expecting to have a great many fine things said to me, to no manner of Purpose. The Defect was surely in your Tools, for I'm confident of the goodness of mine, which wou'd infallibly have explain'd your Inclinations, had you taken care to signify them properly. And I must reproach you thus far, that had you thought what you wrote to me material for me to know, you had not been so unseasonably negligent on this occasion.

Adieu.[134]

It surely did the forty-three-year-old suitor no good to hear that he had defective tools, but he persisted with the cipher. By mid-July it had begun to function, yet still the wily Sabina would make no firm response to his gushing overtures. Byrd revealed an awareness of his age when he pleaded with her, "I wou'd give half an Age of useless life, for the pleasure of conversing half an hour with my Dear Sabina."[135] Sabina, however, was playing hard to get. Either she had only been playing games with Byrd or she had a good sense of her market value and was determined to hear Byrd's bid plainly put to her father.

TO VERAMOUR.

July 10, 1717.

I am surpriz'd to find you so wretchedly mistaken in the construction which you put upon my innocent letters. I swear by the constancy of my sex, that I meant not to indulge your odious complements to me. T'is strange a woman cant write a civil Epistle to a man, but instantly tis understood by his vanity to be a licence to say soft things to her. Had you taken due heed to the good wishes which I sent you in my last, you wou'd have understood it to be a farewell, and consequently a Prohibition for you to write any more. But since you were so stupid as not to apprehend my Plain meaning in that matter, I am forc't to take this harsher Remedy of returning your last letter unopen'd. Tis true I thought you a man of honour, or I shou'd not have taken upon me the part that so ill becomes a Woman: but instead of answering you my self, I had beseech'd the old Gentleman to do it for me. Sure you think me a very odd Nymph, when you imagin I wou'd carry on a secret correspondence with any Gentleman. That wou'd look as if I intended to dispose of my own person, whereas I'm determin'd to be carry'd to market by my Father. However that you may not hang your self quite, I assure you I have no disrespect for you, tho I dont read your Billet but send it back with the seal unbroken. I am oblig'd to you for your care about the Post, but I was just as cautious as you; in that we jumpt, tho we disagree so widely in other matters. Adieu. and be wise if you can.[136]

In the language both of the eighteenth and of the twentieth century, she was a bitch. In the meaning of the eighteenth century she was also a flirt, an almost equally severe term. Sabina was playing a hard-eyed game of courtship which would determine her future master. Unless she survived marriage to become a widow, she would never know such independence again. She was plainly determined to enjoy her independence by playing with William Byrd, whom she seems to have been holding in reserve in case a younger and more distinguished suitor did not appear. This much was accepted practice in eighteenth-century courtship, which was often likened to war. What was not accepted was the edge of cruelty with which she persistently led on a middle-aged man and then evaded him.

Byrd replied, "I'm sorry at my soul I have been so unlucky as to offend the lovely Sabina. . . . No I cou'd as soon design my own Destruction as any thing that might bring a stain upon the dear Damsel I love."[137] He continued in this doddering vein through eight more enciphered letters in the summer and fall of 1717 until they began again to be returned "undecypher'd" in October 1717. "If my Dearest Sabina could but figure to her self half the torment I feel, for her haveing sent back my letters, she wou'd never find in her heart to do so cruel a thing: but wou'd condescend to suffer a Passion which she won't return. . . . Nothing in nature can stop that intire inclination, but what at the same time must stop my Pulse. . . . I beg most earnestly that you'll be so good as to permit me to make you one Proposal . . . to make you the happiest of Women: but if you shou'd be so hard-hearted as to refuse me, I must the very short time I have to live be the unhappiest of men."[138]

By January 1718 Sabina began momentarily to be interested in Byrd. In the one letter she wrote that rings true, she replied that it was above all Byrd's constant and persistent disguising of his intentions in secret, enciphered letters which irritated her. She asked him now to pursue "the forms" by making a proposal in plain English to her father. She did so with characteristic brutality.

TO VERAMOUR.
January 23, 1718.

Supposeing this Billet to be as Romantick as all the rest, I did not think it worth a sincere womans while to decypher it. I desire you if I have any Interest in your heart, not to pursue your address in this distant manner: but if you must attaque me, let it be in the forms. A woman is no more to be taken than a Town by randome shot at a distance, but the Trenches must be open'd, and all the approaches must be regular, and rather than abide the last Extremity, tis possible the Garrison may capitulate, especially if terms be offer'd that are honorable. Tis a sad case when a swain is so intolerably dull, that his mistress must prescribe her own method of being taken; however supposeing this blindness to proceed from pure Passion, I will befreind it so far as to tell you, that my Brother is intirely in my Interest: and if you can get into

his good graces, he may negociate this important affair
betwixt us to both our satisfactions. I expect you'll
make the most of this hint, for when a mistress gives her
Lover advice, she never forgives him if he dont follow it.
Adieu.[139]

By February 1718, the complaisant Byrd was in a fever of
preparation chronicled in his diary as well as in his letters.
With the help of Sabina's brother-in-law, Lord Dunkellin, he
drew up a list of his assets for presentation to Sabina's skeptical father. By this time Sabina had been again converted to
secrecy, and was giving Byrd detailed advice in cipher on preparing this application to her father. In the application, submitted late in February, Byrd came right to his most vulnerable point: "Fearing lest the distance of my Estate from
hence, might be liable to objection I had not the courage to
make a Regular Proposal. However . . . I think it my duty to
explane my circumstances to you, and humbly intreat your
consent." He then went on to list his 43,000 acres and two
hundred negroes, which yielded a clear income of between
£1,500 and £1,800 a year. Save for dowries for his two daughters, Byrd would settle the whole estate on his marriage.
There was no mention of the Parke debts, still mounting toward a total of more than triple his annual income, or of his
desperate attempt to borrow another £10,000 from the Perrys
in order to impress Sabina's father. In a rather sad note, Byrd
offered as references Ned Southwell, who had married Lady
Betty Cromwell from under his nose, and Sir John Perceval,
who was soon to scan Byrd's limitations so sympathetically
in his opinion on Byrd's old portrait of Sir Robert Southwell.[140] These were all the social currency Byrd had to offer.
Observing that his family was an old English family, he vol-
unteered to stay in England if he should be allowed to marry
Miss Smith.

In the days immediately after this presentation Byrd's letters began to take on an agonized tone. "Therefore my dear-

est Angel write often I conjure you, and when you don't write,
be so good as to bestow a tender thought upon me. O why
may I not see you? why won't you trust me with that happiness? what can you apprehend from him whose tenderness
and fidelity wou'd make him all obedience? . . . In the name
of good nature how can you refuse this Blessing to the man
that wou'd dye for you? . . . Lord how hard it is to fetter down
Love to the vexatious Rules of Discretion?"[141]

But Commissioner Smith had already given his reply in a
remark then relayed by his daughter that "an Estate out of
this Island appears to him little better than an Estate in the
moon, and for his part he wou'd not give a Bermigham groat
for it."[142] By the middle of March this dutiful daughter, who
was never very interested in Byrd save in inflicting pain on
him, sought to end his suit. This time her curtness was mercy
in disguise.

> You perceive that your fortune cant be made agreable to
> my Father, without which there can be no hopes of his
> consent, which I give you my word will intirely govern
> mine. . . . I must desire you if you have the least value in
> the world for me never to write at all, and by complying
> with my desire in this particular you will certainly ob-
> lige etc.[143]

Byrd refused to give up. For the rest of March he hung
about in places where he might catch a glimpse of his Sabina.
He wrote her letters in English begging with an almost mad
insistence for her to notice him at all. "God grant you may
not live to reproach your self when you hear of my TRAGEDY
however if after all you shou'd give away your heart to a
happyer man than my self he must expect to give proof of one
good quality besides his Estate. Dont forbid me to write nor
dont send back my letters for I am too near distraction to
obey either." Distraction in the language of the eighteenth
century implied mental illness. The implication was correct.
Byrd's personality was disintegrating, costing him all power

of judgment.[144] On March 30, 1718, Mary Smith had to call in her lawyer to ask Byrd to stop bothering her. On March 31, Byrd wrote in his diary, "Then came Mr. Orlebar with a message from Miss Smith that I should not trouble her any more with my letters or addresses, and returned my letter that I wrote last to her. I was very much concerned but said little to him, but when he was gone I cried exceedingly."[145]

Byrd resumed the sterile routines of the diary but Miss Smith remained in his dreams. In April he heard that she had agreed to marry Sir Edward Des Bouverie, knight, member of Parliament, and eldest son and heir of Sir William Des Bouverie, who had himself been a distinguished and wealthy leader of the London mercantile community. When the sons of merchants achieved such distinctions they became honored as gentlemen, and the younger Des Bouverie was out of Byrd's class in status as well as in estate. Stung, Byrd began to write to Sabina again, pleading with her, begging her, dwelling on what he saw as his chief vulnerability, his estate in Virginia. "I confess I did repine at its distance because it displeas'd [your father]; tho in truth there is no difference between an Estate in Virginia and in Middlesex as long as I receive the Profits of it in London. . . . For Gods sake employ your powerfull Interest with him. . . . I intreat you my Dearest M S, shew this generous Instance of your Pity and my Heart will burn with everlasting gratitude and affection for you. Adieu my dearest Angel may all the stars in their Courses join their Influence to make you perfectly and unchangeably happy." Her only reply was further pleas to desist.[146]

At the end Byrd turned bitter and threatened to expose Miss Smith as a cheat who had encouraged his proposals and so could not in honor marry another. He claimed that her own father, on hearing of her behavior, had called her both a "bitch" and, finally, a "jilt."[147] On May 8, Sir Edward Des Bouverie visited Byrd to order him to desist. Des Bouverie also made it known about town that he would challenge Byrd to a duel if he did not.[148] This threat put an end to the ignominy. A lonely, aging man, hiding himself in cipher, had pursued in the youthful form of Mary Smith the goddess of that success he had sought all his life. But he had picked a woman who could not decipher him. She did not even want to. As he saw it, he had been rejected yet again because he was a colonial, and now his secret mind had begun to tell him that he was also too old. Certainly too old to fight a duel with Sir Edward Des Bouverie. All the most powerful themes of William Byrd's life had culminated in agony in London in the spring of 1718.

The breakdown of Byrd's life was accelerated by this disaster, which expressed itself all too clearly in his diary and love letters. His initial reaction in 1718–1719 was to regress still further into the behaviors of his youth. He began once again to write in the artificially "witty" genres of the early London years. He had sought reassurance in these once and he now sought it again. His portrait of his patron, the duke of Argyll, as "Duke Dulchetti" was fully as tedious as his earlier portrait of Sir Robert Southwell and much less truthful. But this time the main genre was poetry, one seldom exercised in his youth. Most of the poems published in "Tunbrigalia, by Mr. Burrard" in 1719 were as inadequate as the prose portraits of his youth and for the same reasons. They were mannered exercises which rarely found the release of true wit.

On the Lady Percival.

Silence were Sin, when, *Percival,* thy Name
Should stand the Monument of lasting Fame.
To speak thy Beauty, tell thy pleasing Air,
With such Perfections as with these compare;
Words were but Wind, for they express no more
Than what the World would say, *They knew before.*
But if good Sense Perfection may define,
Let Conversation shew how great's thy Mind.[149]

Many of the writings of 1718–1719 and of subsequent
years up to 1725 also showed a hatred of women rarely seen
in the earlier writings. Yet in this one particular Byrd achieved
a kind of catharsis. In one of the few pieces of true wit he had
yet managed, a poem evidently written in 1718 and later
turned into a song by John Gay, he found a way to express and
so perhaps to master his increased hostility toward women.

A SONG

Sabina with an Angels face,
    By Love ordain'd for Joy,
Seems of the Syren's cruel Race,
    To Charm and then destroy.

With all the arts of Look and dress,
    She fans the fatal fire:
Thro Pride, mistaken oft for Grace,
    She bids the Swain expire.

The God of Love inrag'd to see,
    The Nymph defy his flame;
Pronounc'd this merciless Decree,
    Against the haughty Dame.

Let Age with double speed oretake her;
    Let Love the room of Pride supply;
And when the Fellows all forsake her
    Let her gnaw the sheets & dy.[150]

Any resolution of Byrd's feelings after his failure with
Sabina was put off by his final political failure in the summer
of 1719. Spotswood had at last broken him. Byrd's friend from
years before, John Campbell, now the duke of Argyll, had managed to keep Spotswood's connections on the Board of Trade
from taking away Byrd's seat on the Council. But the Board's
price was that Byrd must go home and apologize to Spots-

wood and that all parties must accept a compromise on the
major issues dividing Council and governor. The most the
Council got out of this was a tacit understanding, but by no
means a guarantee, that for the near future Spotswood would
appoint only councillors to the court of oyer and terminer.
Since Spotswood by now had had a few of his friends appointed to the Council itself, this understanding did not in
fact limit his potential control of the new court. Further, all
parties knew that the governor had been confirmed by the
Board of Trade in his legal right ultimately to appoint whom-
soever he chose, whether of the Council or not, as judges of
oyer and terminer, so that this issue was by no means resolved
to the Council's satisfaction. Byrd had no choice but to accept this compromise, since to refuse was to lose his last
high office, to wit, his father's place on the Council, but it
also meant that he would never become governor of Virginia
or of any colony. The powers that be in London were heartily
sick of the endless wrangling over Virginia. At the center of
this wrangling, from their point of view, had been the persistently self-serving Mr. Byrd. They thought that by sending
him home they could have peace in Virginia. They would
never turn to him for further positions of trust. Nor would he
seriously seek such positions. It was unfair, as the issues
which both the Council and the Burgesses held against Spotswood were sometimes legitimate ones.[151] Yet there was a
rough justice in sending Byrd home to end his stirring of an
already boiling pot.

He faced going home in shame and in some fear. Using language in which he described himself as a convicted felon, he
wrote to Argyll, "[As] the time now draw's near for my trans-
portation, [I] repeat my humble request to your Grace for the
letter you was pleasd to say you woud write to Arroganti
[Spotswood]. I was so happy as to be in that gentlemans good
graces the 2 first years of his government, but after that he
grew out of humour with me . . . and from thenceforth he en-
deavourd to make my post uneasy to me." Byrd then denies

*William Byrd II, probably c. 1720s (see page 38, above).
Courtesy of Virginia Historical Society Collections.
Photograph courtesy of The Colonial Williamsburg
Foundation.*

that his aim was ever to remove Spotswood but only to seek justice. The rest of the letter is a plea that the duke intervene with Spotswood to prevent further retribution against Byrd on his return to Virginia. "As he hath done his utmost to remove me from the Council, so I expect he will continue to do me all the ill turns he can when I come into his dominions." He had already made the same plea to the Board of Trade. To Argyll, Byrd also begged assistance in forcing Spotswood to let him return to England as soon as the "reconciliation" ordered by the Board of Trade had been made.[152] Sent home by the Board of Trade, Byrd could not feel secure in Virginia either, so he would return to England if he could get Argyll to persuade the disapproving Board to allow him to come back. He was truly a man without a home. He had pursued his ambitions very nearly to personal and political oblivion.

VIII

The disasters of 1714–1719 had at times threatened the disintegration of Byrd's personality. The London diary and the letters to Sabina are the works of a hollow-eyed, "distracted" man who feels life slipping away from him. As it was. Burdened with increasing debts, his wife dead, his fondest marital and political hopes had been crushed. In the end he had to crawl back home in shame to a country in which he could no longer feel at ease before begging to return to an England which did not want him. If he had ever reflected on his schoolboy dreams, all the pain of his failure would have flooded in on him. He probably did, for as he sailed to Virginia late in 1719 he had terrible dreams of the potential deaths of his daughters, the only close family he had left, and of destruction.[153]

But there was a resilience to William Byrd's personality and to his station in life which had preserved him from madness. From 1719 on he began to mature. Ultimately he drew back from the brink of exiled sterility and became a major figure in Virginia life. He matured also as a Virginia man of letters. The sources of this unexpected maturity were not clear, but Byrd still had significant assets. He had always had a certain cushion of wealth which made his status as a Virginia gentleman secure. His legal education still guaranteed him respect on the Council provided he kept his aspirations within reasonable limits. There was also a strong presumption that his father's place on the Council belonged to him so long as he could control his ambitions and accept Spotswood's ire. Should Spotswood eventually retire, Byrd would once again sit securely on the Council. He still had prospects for a respectable though not dazzling marriage. Qualities developed in his childhood further assisted Byrd in achieving stability. He still had exquisite manners. He was adaptable. He was, as he well knew, likable, and he had for all of his life cultivated a calm detachment. When he left England in 1719 this detachment had nearly been stripped from him, but in Virginia, the scene of his earlier successes, it would slowly return.

The stabilizing rhythms of the diary surely helped as well, for it had now been his counselor for at least ten years. When he had broken down in tears after the interview with Miss Smith's lawyer, he had confessed his despair to the diary. It had served him in the face of death and now of defeat. While still organized around his encoded self, the diary was more than a mirror. It had become a friend.

Even with these assets, maturity was a slow process. It would require considerable help from circumstance. The process seems to have begun on his return to Virginia in 1719–1721. It would be delayed by a return to England, partly to escape from Spotswood's wrath, partly to find a wife, from 1721 to 1726. But even back in England there would be progress. By the time he returned to Virginia in 1726 he was ready to become recognizably a different man within the bounds of the original personality still embodied in his diary. By 1728 he became a man capable of facing his limitations. He learned to deal with his actual place in the world. He became capable of growth within that limited role, and in time was able to deal with his role as a set of flexible metaphors in which he was comfortable. His texts changed and grew accordingly. He would never entirely stop throwing precepts convulsively at a rigid set of ambitions formed in his lonely childhood. He would never stop being inwardly shy. But of the worst moments of his earlier life, only the diary would remain, and it, like his life, would be changed. It was something of a miracle that a man in his late forties as utterly a failure as Byrd had become by 1719, could not only avoid madness but eventually emerge into the sunlight of a late maturity.

IX

When William Byrd embarked for Virginia on December 13, 1719, he was nearly as naked as a man in his position could be. His debt to the Perrys of Perry and Lane, in return for their settling of the Parke debt, had grown so large he could not hope to pay it off for years. Old Micajah Perry, head of the firm, would die within eighteen months, turning control over to his namesake grandson. Micajah the younger would prove a far more aggressive pursuer of debts.[154] No English bride had come to Byrd's rescue with a large settlement, nor would one in the future. Politically Byrd was in danger of losing his seat on the Council unless his reconciliation with Spotswood was convincing to the Board of Trade. Even if it was, Spotswood might seek to rob him of his political influence in Virginia. For this reason Byrd had pleaded with the duke of Argyll to help him return to England. Forebodings of a dreadful future were plainly on his mind. Small wonder then, as he undertook a winter voyage during which his life itself would be at stake, that Byrd was "terrified."[155] The indications are that this was a cumulative terror deeper than that usually evoked by a voyage.

Already in November as he had packed and "laid up his chariot" in storage before the voyage, Byrd had shown signs of nervousness. His sexual restlessness had begun to increase. He had engaged two young maidservants for the voyage, both of whom he would attempt to seduce. One of these women may have been Annie Wilkinson, who was already becoming his sexual plaything in the months after Miss Smith had cast him off. On the boat the quarters were to be too close for sexual byplay but in Virginia "Annie" was to become perforce his chief sexual object. His guilty sexual play with her was to increase steadily after the voyage, reaching a peak in the final weeks of his eighteen-month stay in Virginia. In the midst of the final acts of his frantic sexual odyssey in London, as he engaged Annie and her companion for the voyage, he had awakened with a start to hear "a terrible noise in the night like a woman crying." This was on November 14, 1719, four years almost to the day since his wife Lucy had died of the smallpox. All through November and early December friends had assembled to see him off, in the long goodbyes of the eighteenth-century voyager, but Byrd had remained restless. He had slept badly, he could not say his prayers.[156]

Shortly after the voyage began in December, the sources of his fears began to emerge. On December 21, a week into the voyage, he reported that he "slept indifferently, being disturbed in my dreams about Westover." A week after this, "I was wakened with something like the apparition of my daughter Evelyn and soon after dreamed she died that moment of the smallpox, which God forbid. I dreamed she died about three o'clock in the morning at London." Still a week afterward, still at sea, he "dreamed that my daughter appeared to me with one hand only, from whence I [judged] that one of my daughters is dead, and because it was the left hand that was left, I concluded that the youngest daughter is alive and the other dead, as I dreamed before." Byrd was not concerned about his life in these dreams, although as they neared shore he was to sleep "indifferently because I had Cape Hatteras in my head."[157] Rather, his initial fears were of the destruction or loss of the only secure things he had left to him, Westover and his daughters. Debt, a failed courtship, and political bankruptcy had taken from William Byrd all his other dreams. He now feared losing the last bastion of his status and of his father's status, the home plantation at Westover. He feared the death of the last person close to him, his eldest daughter, Evelyn. These were all Byrd had left that were certain.

Yet this same voyage began a curiously liminal period in Byrd's life. On the voyage itself and for the next eight years he would float neither here nor there in terms of his status and in this precise sense was in a "liminal" state. He would emerge from these indeterminate years a more mature man. Where anyone as naked as Byrd was in 1719 and 1720 got the leverage eventually to mature is almost beyond grasping, but the process may have begun during this initial voyage to Virginia to make his peace with Spotswood. Perhaps Byrd was shocked by the depths to which he had sunk. Certainly he was ashamed by his sexual desperation and haunted by his debts. Perhaps, too, there was a certain sense of freedom entailed in his losses. Liminality—the loss of all conventional status, as in this gentleman-turned-felon "transported" to Virginia in nightmares over the loss of his last possessions—has a way of freeing the victim from the constraints of convention. Old roles may be cast off, or recast. No one ever needed this liberation more than William Byrd. It is indisputable that he arrived in Virginia in his own mind little more than a man. Perhaps this gave him the freedom to begin to change. Then, too, there was the further euphoria of discovering on arrival in January 1720 that his knowledge, charm, and estates were all still good social currency in Virginia. Within limits, he was a welcome political ally against

Spotswood. This process of loss and self-discovery which took place on the voyage of 1719 and after his arrival in Virginia in 1720 probably ran deeper still. Having lost all, he may have finally rid himself of his father's injunctions to improve according to the lights and advantages he had received. He had in fact nearly ruined himself along with these advantages. Having lost all, he was free of his father's voice. He was free to set out to win it all back. William Byrd may have stood on the Virginia shore in 1720, stripped and remade, potentially a new man.[158]

But it was a long process to turn this fresh nakedness, however euphoric it may have been, into maturity however limited. In a process fully as hypothetical as Byrd's childhood at Felsted School, it took the next eight years to mature this "new" man at all. Stripped of his pretensions by the Board of Trade, he would float nervously in Virginia for eighteen months until the summer of 1721, always anxious of Spotswood. He would return to England again to seek a bride, then after five years return to Virginia in 1726, keeping his rooms in London just in case. Only after 1728 did he give up these rooms to settle permanently in Virginia. Similarly, the process of maturity concealed within these years from 1720 to 1728 was slow, contradictory, and partial. Only in retrospect, after 1728, did it become clear that Byrd had passed from the world of precept to that of living metaphor; that he had ceased the obsessive pursuit of rigid ambitions aimed at making him an English gentleman and had become a Virginia gentleman, politician, and writer. In the long perspective only can it be seen that he had accepted himself for what he was and learned to live by these metaphors. It would be easier not to narrate these liminal years, from 1720 to 1728, and to pass on to their result in the form of Byrd's texts, but so many clues to his eventual maturity lie in these years that their story must be told even if speculatively.

Anxiety was the dominant mood from the moment Byrd stepped off his ship on February 4, 1720, until he reembarked for London more than eighteen months later. He nervously greeted friends until a message from the governor "put an end to all my thoughts of peace." On the same day, "I wondered Mr. Clayton came not among my visitors but it was for fear of the Governor which kept several other gentlemen from coming."[159] This theme ran all through Byrd's visit, despite a violent reconciliation with Spotswood late in April. Anxiety pervaded Byrd's role in the Council's continuing effort to undermine Spotswood politically within Virginia after this reconciliation. It emerged in a final confrontation when, in December 1720, as Byrd was preparing to return to England, Spotswood brought the processes of government to a halt in an effort to force the House of Burgesses to limit Byrd's jurisdiction as their agent in England for Indian affairs. The governor was determined not to let the Burgesses give the "implacable" Byrd free rein to criticize any aspect of the administration he pleased.[160] The constant tension which reached a peak in such encounters sent Byrd into tizzies of insecurity. In August 1720, two days after he had applied his influence to elect Burgesses hostile to Spotswood, Byrd escaped into fantasy when he "dreamed the King's daughter was in love with me." Little more than a week after the confrontation with Spotswood in December 1720 over his commission as agent for the Burgesses, he "dreamed I was very dear to the King and he made me Secretary of State and I advised with my Lord Oxford how to manage that great office."[161] These were, however, virtually the last such dreams he was to dream.

More often the escape from tension was sexual. The dream about the king's daughter really encapsulates both of Byrd's escapes, fantasies of power, and sexual release. The next night he "dreamed I made love to a young sister and made her in love with me while I intended to get the older."[162] The habit begun in London, of seeking sexual diversion from his cares and then guiltily regretting it, became obsessive in Virginia in these tense months. Byrd "committed uncleanness"

with Annie or kissed Annie till he "spent," "for which God
forgive me," almost daily in some weeks.[163] In his restless
search for consolation Byrd began to fondle black women,
something rare previously in his life. His conscience sent
him in preference to white women, however, and he sought
them out wherever he could. On March 11, 1721, he "walked
with Mrs. Duke to the landing and when I returned I found
Jenny P-r-s [in this case probably white] come to bring back
my bottle. . . . I kissed her and felt her breasts for about two
hours and then she walked off." Two days later he "walked to
the old plantation to meet Jenny P-r-s but the whore did not
come." A few weeks later he tried again, unsuccessfully. In
Williamsburg, "I walked a little to pick up a woman and
found none."[164] Virginia had not come far enough, evidently,
to offer the resources of London. So instead Byrd made a fool
of himself by flirting with respectable ladies after church.
"After church I invited Mrs. Duke and Mrs. [Hunt], Colonel
Eppes and one Mr. G-ing who came to court Mrs. [Hunt]. . . .
I kissed Mrs. [Hunt] several times and she was not very unwilling." Despite his agonized resolves to stop, he could not.
By early 1721 such episodes had reached a crescendo. His relations with his maidservants had also become public knowledge. "The Captain [Wharwood], John Blair, and I stayed and
drank punch till the Captain and I had almost quarreled
about the women that I brought with me."[165]

By the spring of 1721, women and wine had been supplemented by pills. Some nights, Byrd could not sleep without
"Anderson's pills."[166] Plainly, he could not stand the stress of
the Virginia politics he had helped create. Indeed, as the final
quarrel with Spotswood over Byrd's mandate as agent for the
Burgesses began to develop in December 1720, Byrd dreamt
for the first time in years of his own death.[167] Political tension, as much as his renewed desire to find an heiress, sent
him back to London the following summer. Once there, he
discovered that not even the majority of the Council trusted
him, as they made another man their agent in a head-on con-

test for the post. It was not long since that some members had voiced suspicion of Byrd's ambitions for the governorship.[168] It all sounded terribly familiar.

Yet in Virginia in 1720 and 1721 and back in London afterward significant changes were taking place within the man. They suggested that the lessons of his mistakes had been learned. If disaster had made Byrd anxious, it seems also to have freed him to accept himself in the reduced role which disaster prescribed for him, that of one Virginia gentleman-politician among many. His chief worry seems to have been whether Spotswood and his debts would leave him even this role. In such acceptance lay the key to his eventual maturity. Acceptance had begun in constraint, when in 1719, under pressure from the Board of Trade, Byrd had "proposed" that he make peace with Spotswood. In the process he had had to deny publicly that he had ever had ambitions to unseat his rival in order to take his place. But sometime between 1719 and 1721 constraint appears to have become voluntary acceptance of his reduced station in life. Or, of what had always been his real station. After this time, save for one wistful inquiry in 1726 and another, motivated by debt, in 1736, Byrd appears to have abandoned his long quest for a governorship.[169] It had brought him only pain. It now threatened to bankrupt him financially and politically. There was no need, no reason to go on.

There is a strong suspicion that the mental transition to reduced ambitions actually began in 1719 on the way to Virginia. Embarking in fear, Byrd had entered Virginia already stripped of all his pretensions. On shipboard, dreaming of the loss of Westover, of his eldest daughter, of everything, he did not know what he could salvage at all. This liminal openness made him terribly vulnerable, hence his anxious fear of Spotswood and of annihilation, and his subsequent reversion to fantasies of political and sexual power. But liminality also relieved him of a lifelong burden of inherited ambition and left him free in the potential openness of his position. Whatever he salvaged from this point on was his own, not his father's. He would begin from nothing to create himself anew. Of course, it was not totally anew, as his worst dreams proved unfounded. He kept Westover, his daughters lived, and he was never removed from the Council. He was not totally new, also, in that he continued all his life to keep his diary. In it he reacted to his anxieties in old ways. But in his sea-born nakedness it must have seemed as if he was being born anew, with all the risks and glories that involves.

In a letter to the earl of Orrery of March 6, 1720, written a few weeks after his arrival, Byrd himself would implicitly describe his voyage in retrospect as a rite of passage. In this letter, he observed that he would remember Orrery's many favors to him in England even if he were to undergo the Indian initiation rite known as "husquenawing," which he depicted as follows:

> This operation is performed upon the Indians of this part of the world at the age of puberty when they commence men, and is in order to make them forget all the follys of their childhood. For this end they are lock't up in a place of security, and the physicians of the place ply them night and morning with a potion that transports them out of their senses, and makes them perfectly mad for six weeks together. When this time is expired, they are kept upon meager dyet for three days, and in that space they return to their understanding, but pretend to have forgot every thing that befell them in the early part of their lives.

From the context it is clear that Byrd was in fact thinking of his voyage across the Atlantic as a rite of initiation which he had already undergone, for his very next words were, "I had no reason to have been terrified [as he had been, for many reasons] at a winters passage."[170] Somewhere in his mind, then, William Byrd seems to have known that he had left behind him, along with the madness of the dreams which accom-

panied his transport across the sea, "the follys" of his childhood and the "early part" of his life. And despite his continuing anxiety, since his arrival in Virginia he had certainly
found no terror in the consequences.

Perhaps the governor had shattered his "hopes of peace"
with a hostile message immediately after his arrival in February, while some gentlemen had not appeared for fear of the
governor, but Byrd had received vast reassurance from his initial reception everywhere else in Virginia. Ill in bed of a nervous complaint, he had recorded with touching gratitude the
stream of old friends and political associates who flocked to
see him on his arrival. On February 6, "After dinner Colonel
Smith [a member of the Council] came to see me. . . . The
Colonel told me all the news. He was so kind as to stay all
night. I ate some chicken broth for supper and was pretty
well, thank God, but could not sit but the only place where I
was easy was abed. I slept pretty well, thank God." Next day,
"Phil Lightfoot [another member of the Council and a very
wealthy man] came to see me and offered me his chariot to go
to Williamsburg tomorrow. I thanked him kindly and accepted his offer. He stayed about two hours and then left me
and went with my landlord to church. I sat up a little while
but could not sit very easy, though I was better, thank God."
The day after, "Mr. Lightfoot and his chariot came. . . . I . . .
took leave of my good landlord and went to Williamsburg and
by the way overtook Major Custis [an oddly, tentatively formal way of describing his brother-in-law and former close
friend] and went to his house where several gentlemen came
to see me." The "several gentlemen" included half the political elite of Virginia, among them the bishop of London's commissary for the Anglican church in Virginia, James Blair, who
was for fifty years the nearest thing to an archbishop Virginia
was to have, a member of the Council, and the éminence
grise of Virginia politics.[171]

The center of such solicitous attentions from his friends,
perhaps in some cases all the more solicitous in their relief at

discovering that their enemy Alexander Spotswood had not been replaced by William Byrd, Byrd had quickly gotten off chicken soup and back into Virginia politics. This wave of acceptance, the small gestures of kindness, the mass attendance on his person, must have been a buoyant experience after the bleak years in London followed by six weeks of despair on the boat. By the time he wrote to Orrery in March, Byrd had been suddenly reborn as a Virginia politician. He had been reborn in the kindness, and in the need, of political allies who welcomed him as one of them even while some of them were to reject him as agent and potential governor. In the long run the lesson could not have been lost on Byrd. He could be reborn provided he accept a realistic context to his ambitions. In accepting the attentions showered upon him in his failure, and he accepted such attentions from his political equals in Virginia with a frequency and warmth never shown before by this proud man, Byrd was implicitly agreeing to be reborn in the capacity of a Virginia politician among his equals. What the Board of Trade had forced him to accept pro forma, and the voyage had probably freed him to reflect upon, this reception had encouraged him to embrace inwardly by its warmth.

In the ensuing months Byrd was to be as unsure in approaching some of his old friends in the neighborhood around Westover as he had been in approaching Virginia politics in Williamsburg. This time he did not take to his bed in frightened illness, and he was plainly touched by the warmth of his reception here as well. Here, too, he soon saw that he had nothing to fear in his new form. On April 6, "I went to dine with Will Kennon, and there Parson Robinson met us and Major Bolling. . . . After dinner we sat and talked till 4 o'clock and then went to Major Bolling's where we drank punch. . . . Mrs. Bolling is a clean, good woman and everybody was very courteous to me." Just as the William Byrd of 1709–1712 had seldom accepted favors from his political equals, so he had never deigned to comment on the courtesy shown him by his social inferiors, preferring instead to command their "respect." But now he was a different man. He was grateful to be treated as a man worthy of courtesy by his old friends and neighbors. Three days later, on April 9, "I got [to Mr. Bland's, for the funeral of a neighbor across the James] about 12 o'clock and soon after there came abundance of company, of both sexes. We had a sermon and everything that was necessary for the occasion. Everybody was very courteous to me and I was the same to everybody."[172] For a desperate man these courtesies were a second rebirth. After the desolation, it was good to be a Virginia squire.

The greatest acceptance was yet to come. Stopping at Williamsburg in February, renewing friendships around Westover in March and April, had all been preludes to the inevitable confrontation with Sir Alexander Spotswood. When it came, on April 29, 1720, it was described in terms of sweet relief.

> I rose about 6 o'clock and read a chapter in Hebrew and some Greek. I said my prayers, and had milk for breakfast. The weather continued dry and clear, the wind west. About ten Mr. Commissary came to my lodgings and we walked to the court and then went into Council where there passed abundance of hard words between the Governor and Council about Colonel Ludwell and Mr. Commissary for about two hours till of a sudden the clouds cleared away and we began to be perfectly good friends and we agreed upon terms of lasting reconciliation, to the great surprise of ourselves and everybody else. The Governor invited us to dinner and entertained us very hospitably and the guns were fired and there was illumination all the town over and everybody expressed great joy. The Governor kissed us all round and gave me a kiss more than other people. We had also a concert of music at the Governor's and drank the necessary healths till 11 o'clock and then we took leave and walked home and said my prayers.

A kiss from the governor was heady stuff for a man who had lived for months in apprehension of losing everything. Here, too, in Spotswood's arms, there was the lesson at its highest peak that reconciliation with authority could come from an acceptance of a limited station. There was a shift implied here, from the authority of Byrd's distant father, telling him constantly to "improve," to the authority of the Board of Trade and the governor, ordering him not to carry improvement too far and offering him secure status if he would be reconciled with his superior. In the governor's extra kiss, this lesson, too, was ultimately a lesson of friendship for a man reborn from oblivion. All the lessons of his return offered Byrd through friendship new life as a Virginia squire and as a member of the Council. This was the sunshine after the clouds had cleared away.[173]

In this mellow light, in the months from May to November 1720, Byrd could be seen in his own diary doing some things he had never done before. Before, his politics had been all display and ambition. They had led him to go beyond even the Council's position on Spotswood. Now he joined his fellow councillors in an orderly, indigenous political opposition to the governor. Before, he had lampooned the Burgesses as if they were far beneath a councillor on his way to becoming governor. But the compromise imposed by the Board of Trade in 1719, by virtually ordering not only Byrd but also the entire Council to get along with the governor (and the governor with them), had left the disgruntled majority of the councillors only one legitimate arena for their political opposition; namely, the House of Burgesses. The Burgesses had not been included in that paralyzing "compromise," and so were still free to act. Moreover, in the face of the Council's initial timidity in coming out against Spotswood and of its selfish concentration on opposing his scheme to dilute their power on the new court of oyer and terminer, the Burgesses had in fact led the wider opposition to Spotswood's program since 1714. In view of these facts, after 1719 the proud magnates of the Council had no choice but to cultivate burgesses sympathetic to the Council's remaining complaints against Spotswood and to try to use the House as its only possible vehicle against the governor. Now, in 1720, William Byrd in turn accepted the new strength of the Burgesses in Virginia politics and joined his fellow opposition councillors in courting their assistance. "After dinner Captain [Henry] Harrison [burgess from Surry County] came and I caused some victuals to be got for him and I ate some roast pigeon with him again [Byrd had just finished his meal of duck but willingly ate a second]. I read to him several of my books of what I had done in England and talked everything over with him, because he was a man of factor in the House of Burgesses."[174]

What a revelation! Byrd, who began his diary strictly eating one dish at a meal, and lampooning burgesses, is now forcing down a second dish in soliciting the favor of a powerful burgess. In the ensuing months Byrd attended the election of burgesses in three counties near him, until his grass-roots political activities came even to the governor's attention. On October 14, 1720, the governor "received me gravely. I told him I had heard he had been told that I had been busy at elections and justified myself from that calumny."[175] The "calumny" was, of course, perfectly true.

Byrd's aim in cultivating the powerful Henry Harrison and in seeing to the election of acceptable burgesses elsewhere along the James was only partly to consolidate the alliance between the Council and the House against Spotswood. He was also seeking their mutual vote to make him agent for Indian affairs for the Burgesses, a post which would get him back to England with £400 in his pocket. This agency would also potentially put Byrd in a position to stir the political pot once again, but fortunately for Byrd, Spotswood put a stop to any renewal of his wildest ambitions by making it clear that no "meddling" in issues other than Indian affairs would be permitted. From all the evidence of Byrd's subsequent behav-

ior, he either took this advice to heart or played an unprecedentedly well hidden role in future efforts to remove and replace Spotswood.[176] Most likely Byrd had been interested in
this limited post only for the very fat salary, which would
help finance his ongoing search for an heiress in London.
Proof of this can be seen in the Council's vote to support
Byrd's position as agent for the Burgesses even though some
councillors were mistrustful of his ambitions and the majority of the members would refuse to make him their general
agent a few months later. The Council evidently saw no danger in Byrd's angling for the specific post of agent for Indian
affairs. As far as they were concerned, he was now playing the
game of Virginia politics within acceptable limits. The governor's warnings were probably not necessary.

Byrd became at least halfway a Virginia politician, then,
playing the role of councillor even to the unprecedented degree of cultivating the Burgesses and making sure that his
ends, the Council's, and the Burgesses' were in harmony. He
abandoned the proud, satirical stance of his youth to dirty his
hands with ordinary politics for the first time in his life. He
left partially the little dimple of ambition in which he had
lived outside of all ordinary history, to enter the stream of
human exchange, and so the history of Virginia. He was at
last not a foolish schoolboy engrossed in the eternal present
of his own inflated ambitions, but a man living among men
in real time, and with an identity he could manage. There
would be relapses, but it was a beginning.

Byrd became a man among real men and women in a deeper
sense during these extraordinary months in Virginia. Before,
between 1709 and 1712, his relations with his slaves had
been rigidly preceptual. While not brutal, he had seen them
as objects of his first mastery of the roles inherited from his
father. Preceptually, as in a book of advice literature, he had
protected them, observed that they "were punished," and
dosed them with medicines. When he went to the quarters it

was as physician, with a rigid schedule of purgings or vomits. But now in 1720, in his nakedness and in his need, William Byrd began to go to the quarters for friendship.

The change came haltingly, inadvertently, in uncertain language in the diary as if Byrd was searching for a formula to describe this new sort of behavior. Where did it begin? It began in the depths of his need, as he returned to Westover late in February 1720, in the deepest hour of his desperation before the great catharsis of the confrontation with Spotswood. He began in a formal manner with his slaves. On February 29, "I inquired into the affairs of my family." On March 2, "saw my sick people." On March 16, "gave audience to my people." Then the rigid pose began to flex. March 18: "At night I read some news and discoursed my people and ate some toast and milk and about nine retired and said my prayers." Suddenly rigid precept had become a flexible metaphor.[177] This gentleman could fulfill his role not by audiencing or by dosing but by casual discourse. In the process objects had become subjects who could discourse back. It was a new human world.

Gropingly, the change survived. On March 23, "I came home and I talked with my people and read some English till 9 o'clock and then retired and said my prayers." Perhaps this was too honest, too homely, for three days later, "I looked over my people." The old role was more comfortable after all. But it did not really meet his needs, so, after a long pause in which the new behavior was suspended or account of it suppressed, on April 16 excuses were swept aside as again, "I talked with my people." There would be regressions, as in an "audience" on April 23, but "discoursing" and more often "talking" with his people came to be Byrd's way of spending his evenings alone at Westover with his slaves. Some of the calm of this man seeking out others in his openness and isolation could be seen from one such evening, in March of 1721. "After dinner I put several things in order till 5 o'clock and then walked to Mrs. Harrison's and sat with her the whole evening till 9 o'clock and then by the light of the moon walked home and talked with my people and about ten said my prayers and retired and slept pretty well."[178]

Both as a politician and as a slave owner, Byrd was entering the real world as a real gentleman, albeit rather more as a Virginia than as an English one. He was being freed from the compulsive ambition formed in his painful childhood. With the ambition went some of the rigid behaviors aimed, or so the boy had thought, at fulfilling that ambition. Byrd was beginning to be free to see himself as only a man. He was free to work with his friends, his allies, even his slaves in the flexible world where people listened to one another, worked together for political ends, and consoled one another, and in so doing expressed the metaphors of their status and condition. Though no doubt he got more consolation from talking to his slaves in his loneliness than they got from him in their continuing slavery. If it was painful to be reborn a real gentleman, free at last to seek consolation from his slaves while stretching the metaphor of gentility to its limits, it was surely more painful still to be a slave whose master set many of the limits of *that* metaphor as well.

All this can be seen in the diary, which as a result of years of tribulation was becoming a somewhat different instrument. It was still in code. It would always be. The routine was still partially there in the Hebrew, the Greek, the prayers, the one-dish meals, the "dance," the "putting myself in order" every morning—this latter habit now more marked than ever—most of which would endure until Byrd's death.[179] But the spaces after ten or eleven in the morning had already been opened up by the jaded routines of the roué in London. That previous frantic search for success or failing that for gratification had long since forced the Latin out of the routine. It had finally also made impossible the ritual invocation of "good health, good thoughts, and good humor thanks be to God Almighty" at the end of each day. By the end of his London stay in 1719 Byrd had barely been able to go on saying his prayers each night. Now, in Virginia in 1720–1721, the spaces opened up by London's sad searchings were suddenly filled up with new activities. True, the sexual searching was progressively worse in these uncertain years of growth. But at the same time came a rich panoply of political involvements, involvements with friends, and with slaves. Less and less are these described in the language of puerile mastery. Rather, they are the rich materials of what scholars have come to think of as an ordinary diary—engrossing politics, warm friendships, long, earnest conversations over wine.[180] Such pastimes are appreciated for their own sake in this changed diary of a changing man, as they far more seldom were in his first diary. The diary is still in part the relic of an old pathology, and the counselor of an anxious man, but it is ever more crowded and lively. Only the nightly conversations with his slaves slowly became routinized, into "talked with my people." But this new part of his regime directly reflected Byrd's need for contact. Through it he replaced the preceptual "good health, good thoughts, and good humor" as the final item in his daily behavioral and emotional encodement of himself with a living metaphor of gentle behavior which depicted this gentleman doing what he needed to do, not what he had to.

But Byrd had more growing to do. It was above all Spotswood's harsh injunction in December 1720 not to "meddle" beyond his mandate from the Burgesses which sent Byrd into a mounting fit of anxiety in the last months of his visit. Whatever his intentions had been in seeking the agency for Indian affairs from the Burgesses, and the Council had approved these intentions, Spotswood's violent reaction recalled all the raw fears of 1719 to Byrd's still vulnerable mind.[181] If he had thought to go to England only to find a rich bride, possibly then to return, his return to live in Virginia now became fully as questionable as it had been in his letter to Argyll in 1719. For the same reason, Spotswood's wrath. As he returned to England in the summer of 1721 everything in William Byrd's life was very nearly as uncertain as it had been when he went to Virginia. The only certain thing was that he was changing.

From all the evidence, once back in London Byrd was not involved in politics outside the bounds of his agency on Indian affairs. Money gave him the strongest reason to stay uninvolved. For, had Byrd once again challenged Spotswood's legitimacy in London, the Board of Trade would surely have supported its governor by removing Byrd from his seat on the Council. He would have lost his agency for the Burgesses as well. Loss of these offices would have cost the indebted Byrd over £600 income in the first year alone.[182] And he had little to gain in return by meddling, as of all the men the Board of Trade might have picked to replace Spotswood, Byrd would have been the last. Administrations might come and go, but troublemakers were never welcome. This was a lesson of force more than of maturity, but Byrd seems to have registered it unmistakably despite the temptations of his renewed access to the seat of power.

For his restraint, Byrd received an unexpected bonus. In April of 1722 Sir Alexander Spotswood was removed as governor of Virginia. Spotswood had taken on one opponent too many. Commissary of the Church James Blair had come to England with Byrd in 1721 to force the governor to leave him secure in his pulpit and his Anglican clergy in theirs despite Spotswood's efforts to exercise his royal prerogative to approve their appointments. In a sudden shift of the political winds, Robert Walpole became prime minister within a year after Blair's arrival, and Blair gained his ear. Spotswood was swept out of office. He was the third governor the doughty Blair had removed.[183] He had done thrice what Byrd could not do once, but Byrd did not complain. It was a gift from heaven.

He could never become governor himself, but if he chose, William Byrd could now return home with honor. He might have embarked right away had he suspected how much honor, but the battle had taken its toll on him. He did not decide to return until 1726, in part a measure of his timidity, but in part because he still had to find a wife.

In February of 1723, in the last of his unsuccessful English courtships, Byrd revealed that he was finally ready to acknowledge his personal limitations as well as his political ones. He began a friendly correspondence with "Minionet" in the spring of 1722. Her identity is unknown. Possibly she was Molly Jeffreys, a girl of gentle family whose chief feature was her ability to read cipher![184] Their correspondence proceeded along jolly enough lines through the spring, summer, and autumn of 1722. Byrd showed rare restraint in his usual efforts to "entertain" the object of his by now rather fatherly affections. The letters moved from topic to topic without tedium. Their mood was witty and friendly. Not a drop of agony tinged the scene even when in August the lady ordered Byrd to write no more. But by November 1722, a simultaneous and much more serious romance with "Charmante," also unidentified, had collapsed when that lady married a man known for his wit. This insult Byrd could scarcely bear. He wrote an angry tirade rejecting wit after the last of Charmante's billets-doux. Seldom able to achieve wit, he had now been defeated by it in a head-on contest. Significantly, save for a rather gentle play on women's susceptibility to superstition, "The Female Creed," written around 1725, William Byrd was virtually never again to exercise any of the witty genres which had characterized his adult life to that point.[185] Here, as in politics, sheer loss forced him to abandon the compulsive behaviors of his youth, and he drew the right lesson.

Rejected, he turned back to "Minionet," to the girl who could read cipher. He made a scarcely disguised plea to her to decipher him.

TO MINIONET.

February the 21, 1722/3.

When I was last happy in the Conversation of the charming Minionet, I threaten'd her with more of my Pictures, and now that Lent begins to draw near, my being as good as my word may be a seasonable mortification. The first I shall submit to her View, is, of a Gentleman who has the honour to be pretty well known to Her, He also knows her so well as to wish her at least as happy as himself. He really resembles his Picture enough to be a good sort of a man, and gives this certain proof of his fine tast, that he absolutely prefers you to Sempronia, Cornelia, Charmante, and all the brighter ornaments of the sex. He cant with all his modesty be asham'd, to confess a passion so fully justify'd by Reason and good sence. I must own indeed that tis a Princely air to carry on a Courtship thus by Picture, but it has this convenience at least, of hideing the confusion and diffidence of a bashfull Lover. However Madam you will have one advantage very unusual in other addresses, that you will here be able to read the Inside of your admirer before hand, whereas most other Ladys dont find that out til tis too late, and the discovery serves no other Purpose but to inform them, that they are miserable without Remedy.

This was followed by a sudden proposal of marriage.

If you cou'd approve of such a Lover, I wou'd be his security you shou'd not find the original exceedingly flatter'd by the Picture. Nay I cou'd Venture to answer yet farther for Him, that he loves you so tenderly, that if you'd but smile upon his Passion, it shou'd be the Endeavour of his whole Life to make you happy. He has a long time felt these tender sentiments, but cou'd never yet muster up Resolution enough to open his Heart to you. He has therefore with much intreaty prevail'd upon me to do it for him and oh that I were master enough of

the gentle art of perswasion, to possess you a little in his
favour. Then I shou'd think my self as happy as the very
man I was pleading for, which wou'd be the happyest of
mortals. May angels guard my Dearest Minionet and in-
cline her to favour the Intercession of etc.[186]

Minionet never replied, so Byrd had to live with one more
rejection. But he had done something extraordinary. He had
sent her "Inamorato L'Oiseaux," written fifteen years before
and never shown to anyone.[187] This honest self-portrait revealed him in all his vulnerability. It confessed his ambition.
It listed his failures. It admitted the sensitivity which lay behind these. It showed the alternations of constraint and gushing revelation which had always plagued him as he ap-
proached the objects of his emotional and social ambitions
and which plagued him now. Minionet did not need to decipher him at all, for he had sent her himself, in plain English.

From this point on, one must regard Byrd as a relatively
mature individual. Whatever the pain it caused him, he had
partially transcended the broad limitations of the personality
laid down in his school days. He had now set aside his child-
ish genres, the witty portrait, the love letter, the poem. He
had earlier stepped partially outside the constraints of the
initial diary of 1709–1712. By 1720 its routine was less en-
compassing and within that attenuated routine he enjoyed
the play of politics, friendship, and conversation more easily,
with less compunction to study himself or show mastery.
With Minionet he had gone the final step outside the boundaries of the shorthand code of the diary to reveal himself to a
woman in English. After nearly ten years of continuous pain,
he was being born into life as a living human being rather
than as a monster of misconstrued ambition. God gives us all
miracles. William Byrd's growth out of precept and with-
drawal and out of the terrible failures these caused into the
painful world of living metaphors, at the age of nearly fifty,
was his miracle. Like all miracles, it was never quite com-

plete. He was still partially caged in his many encodements. He would never let the diary go. Debt, and anxiety, would never entirely leave him. But he was ready to begin a new life within these limits.

The first positive step toward a new life was a sensible marriage. This Byrd accomplished in May 1724, marrying Maria Taylor. She was the handsome daughter of the late Thomas Taylor of Kensington, probably a merchant. Byrd seems to have been chiefly delighted that she spoke Greek. His one surviving letter to her is in this language, perhaps for him still another cipher, but it seems to have been above all a practical marriage. Byrd was fifty, she twenty-five, both were too old to stay single if they intended to marry at all. Of Maria's promised dowry of £1,000, not a huge sum, Byrd may never have seen a penny. Like Lucy's before it, Maria's dowry seems to have disappeared into the folds of a peculiar family. It was not from all the evidence a passionate marriage, and it established devastatingly Byrd's low position in English society, but Maria bore him three daughters and a son between 1725 and 1729. He was no longer alone to "play the fool" with Annie or be rejected by prospective brides.[188] Maria was the foundation of his coming stability.

The wisest move of all was Byrd's return to Virginia in the summer of 1726. It seems to have been half-accidental, but it was also a product of a changed man. In 1723 his daughter Evelyn had been pursued by a rake of a nobleman, which had angered Byrd.[189] He was attached to Evelyn, as his dreams had revealed, and in fact she would never marry. He may have removed to Virginia partly to "protect" her. But Maria had by 1725 borne their first daughter, Anne, and Byrd may have guessed that the large tobacco crop of the new season would soon cause prices on the European markets to fall drastically. If he were to pay off his debts and to provide for his increasing brood in the face of a falling income from tobacco, he would have to economize. As he put it once he was back in Virginia: "Neither could I sit down quietly under so great a disadvantage [as losing his friend Orrery's company], but for the good of my children. There are so many expences in England, that there is no laying up any thing for them. But here [in Virginia] I can live in great luxury, without being any thing out of pocket, and can save great part of what my effects produce on this side the water. Thus prudence has for once got the better of a very strong inclination, which has happened so seldome to me, that I may be allowed to boast of it."[190]

Boast he might have. It was a sober suitor turned reformed family man who set out to guard his estate in a way he never had, by returning at last to Virginia. Having received the blessing of Spotswood's removal and having confessed himself to Minionet and married Maria, he was now returning after a lifetime of uncertainty to cultivate his only remaining garden. He kept his rooms in London for three more years, but these were eventful years which convinced Byrd once and for all, for reasons far more than financial, that Virginia was now his proper home. In it, a matured man in his fifties would grow to full stature.

X

Sometime between his return in June 1726 and late 1728, William Byrd finally caught his stride as a Virginia gentleman. Having taught himself to accept the realities of his situation, he proceeded to make the most of those realities virtually until the day of his death.

At first his protests about enjoying Virginia were defensive. As he revealed, it was financial pressures which had finally brought him back. Although his new prudence had recognized these necessities, a previous less practical Byrd still longed for the social mirrors he had left behind. This gave his acceptance of his fate a faintly hollow ring. Yet there was sincere pride as well. As he put it in another letter to Orrery, "The beautifull bloom of our spring when we came ashore, gave Mrs. Byrd a good impression of the country." Then in a telling revelation, he confessed that Virginia had become a participant in his maturity. "Your Lordship will allow it to be a fair commendation of a country, that it reconciles a man to himself, and makes him suffer the weight of his misfortunes, with the same tranquility he bears with his own frailtys."[191] With remarkable consciousness, Byrd was describing essentially the process begun on his visit to Virginia in 1720–1721 and now being completed on his return. The beauty of the land and the warmth of his welcome to Virginia had twice given Byrd a way to overcome his misfortunes and increasingly to accept his own limitations. One suspects that in 1726 he had actually been welcomed back as a bit of a hero for leading the way toward Spotswood's removal. In this remark as in his remarks on prudence Byrd revealed that he knew he was a changed man and he articulated the process by which the change had occurred. Necessity, in the form first of the Board of Trade (in 1719) and then of financial pressure (in 1726), had simply driven Byrd into the process of reconciliation with himself and with Virginia which had matured him.

Later in the same letter to Orrery, Byrd launched into a great panegyric on his new life in Virginia in a powerful blend of creativity, resentment, and nostalgia.

Like one of the patriarchs, I have my flocks and my herds, my bond-men and bond-women, and every soart of trade amongst my own servants, so that I live in a kind of independance on every one, but Providence. However tho' this soart of life is without expence yet it is attended with a great deal of trouble. I must take care to keep all my people to their duty, to set all the springs in motion, and to make every one draw his equal share to carry the machine forward. But then tis an amusement in this silent country, and a continual exercise of our patience and oeconomy.

Another thing my Lord, that recommends this country very much, we sit securely under our vines, and our fig-trees without any danger to our property. We have neither publick robbers nor private, which your Lordship will think very strange, when we have often needy governours, and pilfering convicts sent over amongst us. The first of these it is suspected have some-times an inclination to plunder, but want the power, and tho' they may be tyrants in their nature, yet they are tyrants without guards, which makes them as harmless as a scold would be without a tongue. Neither can they do much injustice by being partial in judgment, because in a supream court, the Council have each an equal vote with them. Thus both the teeth and the claws of the lion are secured, and he can neither bite nor tear us, except we turn him loose upon ourselves. I wish this was the case of all His Majesty's good subjects, and I dare say your Lordship has the goodness to wish so too.

Then we have no such trades carried on amongst us, as that of house-breakers, highway-men, or beggers. We can rest securely in our beds with all our doors and windows open, and yet find every thing exactly in place the next morning. We can travel all over the country, by night and by day, unguarded and unarmed, and never meet with any person so rude as to bid us stand. We have no vagrant mendicants to seize and deaften[?] us wherever we go, as in your island of beggars. Thus my Lord we are very happy in our Canaan, if we could but forget the onions, and flesh-pots of Egypt. There are so many temptations in England to inflame the appetite, and charm the senses, that we are constant to run all risques to enjoy them. They always had I must own too strong an influence upon me, as your Lordship will belive when they could keep me so long from the more solid pleasures of innocence, and retirement.[192]

The panegyric was also a farewell to his old life. Wistfully, in his next letter to Orrery,[193] Byrd flirted with the governorship of Virginia, Spotswood's replacement having by now died, then abandoned his past save in nostalgia.

Three events ripened Byrd's commitment to his new role as advocate of his country. In September 1727, William Gooch arrived in Virginia as governor. Byrd said of him, "By great accident we have a very worthy man [as governor]. It is Major Gooch, . . . a very just man, and has a reasonable share of good sense, good-nature and good breeding."[194] Gooch was to remain governor of Virginia until well after Byrd's death in 1744. Byrd never altered his initial opinion. The secret of Gooch's long life as governor, however, as of Byrd's respect, was that by and large he let Virginians govern Virginia. Gooch's master, Sir Robert Walpole, in power most of these years, was satisfied with this policy because it kept the colony quiet.[195] But within Virginia Gooch became a symbol of Virginians' triumph over the stubborn policies of three preceding governors, Nicholson, Andros, and Spotswood. It had, after all, been the opposition of a wide spectrum of Virginia politicians, and in the latter case above all the stubborn resistance of the Burgesses from 1716 to 1720, which had enabled Commissary James Blair to administer the death stroke to each of these governors in succession. Gooch appeared to have learned the lesson. So low a profile did he keep that Byrd could say of his office in an essay published, admittedly, only in German-Swiss and to attract settlers, that the governor was no more than the equal of any of the gentlemen councillors of Virginia. As he put it, "The opinion of each member [of the Council] is of as much importance as that of the governor, and they can contradict him freely . . . when he desires to overstep his prescribed duty." At another point Byrd equated the Council with the House of Lords in England. What satisfaction that must have given William Byrd. If he could not be governor, then he could be the political equal of a diffident English governor in a system which dis-

tributed power widely. It seems scarcely to have troubled him
that that power in fact was increasingly in the hands not of
the Council but of the House of Burgesses.[196] He was now a
Virginian and it was Virginia power.

It was under Gooch, in December of 1727, that Byrd was
appointed with the approval of the Burgesses and Council as
one of Virginia's boundary commissioners to run the line between their colony and North Carolina. This was a distinction and an opportunity for adventure which was to change
Byrd's life. It would give him a new genre and a new vision of
Virginia's future. But most immediately it enabled him to
do something Spotswood had done, to gain glory by leading an expedition to the west.[197] So some of the widely dis-
tributed power in this indigenous political system devolved
very quickly back on councillor Byrd in the form of glory.
That seems to have reconciled him to his place in the local
system of power fully as much as did Gooch's diffidence.

Finally, in subsequent years Gooch as governor and Byrd
as a senior councillor were to lead a long battle against the
efforts of London tobacco merchants led by Micajah Perry
the younger to make all the Virginia gentry's assets subject
to seizure for debts owed in Britain. The duel between Byrd
and Perry over the Parke debts thereby came to be writ large
across the face of the Atlantic. Perry as alderman and eventual lord mayor of London sat in the House of Commons for
the City. Byrd was by now second in seniority only to ancient
Commissary Blair on the Virginia Council of State. Byrd and
the Virginians lost the battle against Perry and the London
merchants in 1732. The Colonial Debts Act made all real estate and slaves in the colonies, previously untouchable unless specifically mortgaged, subject to seizure for any debts
owed in Britain. The Virginians were to lose further battles in
their war with the London merchants, but Byrd's position
of leadership in this political war must have given him deep
satisfaction. As the war went on, he and other Virginians retaliated against Alderman Perry by denying him their to-

bacco, and the firm of Perry and Lane began to founder. Byrd went on paying his debts to Perry with this grim satisfaction. From 1727 to 1732, then, in the process of his successful relationship with Gooch, in his role in running the dividing line with North Carolina, and in his leadership in the battle against the London merchants, William Byrd finally became the Virginia politician he could have been all along. By the 1730s his letters came to be full of schemes for improving his estate, Virginia, and the empire.[198] It was as if a vast energy had been liberated.

XI

It is this William Byrd who created the texts of his late life, largely written between 1729 and 1740, when he was between the ages of fifty-five and sixty-six. Through these texts, he became the Virginia author he was to be known as to all posterity. His two histories of the dividing line between North Carolina and Virginia were hard-won achievements.

When Byrd began writing his histories sometime after 1728 he had not fully exercised his creative urges for some years. When he had rejected the compulsive ambitions of his youth, he had rejected by and large the "witty" poems, portraits, and overwrought love letters which, with the early diary, had been the creations of that ambition. After Charmante had rejected him for a true wit early in 1722, neither in London nor thereafter in Virginia had he systematically practiced these genres. Only the essay "The Female Creed" had escaped him, in 1725, and thereafter scarcely so much as a lampoon. The diary itself had changed as early as 1720 and had perhaps become a more satisfying document. It was no longer so compulsive a mirror of the rigid precepts of his childhood ambition. It was still less the record of a local mastery seen as the first step toward a glorious future as governor. Rather, the

diary had become primarily what it had been in a lesser degree even from the beginning, a counselor.[199] As the record of
Byrd's satisfactions in the metaphors of Virginia politician,
neighbor, and slave owner, the diary was also the mirror of
his growing maturity. He could flex these metaphors sufficiently to allow himself to solicit the help of a burgess, to be
grateful for his friends' attentions, and to value talking with
his slaves. He was secure enough to transform these metaphors of his newly reduced station and to record them being
transformed in his diary. But, while he and his diary had
broken free from the book-learned rigidities of his youth,
this new diary was possibly still less than satisfying as an ar-
tistic expression of Byrd's new life.

Byrd needed an outlet. He needed a new literary mirror for
a new maturity of which he was aware.[200] Indeed, he was a
master now in a much more profound sense than he had been
as a callow youth in 1709. He was a Virginia gentleman
by virtue of his ability to transform the metaphors of that
station. As such he was above all a Virginia politician who
went beyond mere posing to be capable of cooperation and
sustained effort, transforming the metaphor of power daily
through action in the context of other human beings. This
was a creative mastery indeed, wrought from disaster and
executed in the real world. Wit was too artificial a genre, and
the diary was too restrictive, adequately to express the play
of this personality.

Running the dividing line between North Carolina and
Virginia in the spring and autumn of 1728 gave Byrd the
largest stage of action he had yet enjoyed. This playing out of
his new mastery, his genuine mastery of Virginia politics
from the governor's office to the coastal swamps and nearly
to the mountains in the west, provided Byrd the occasion
for exercise of a new creative genre. Lowering his creative
sights as he had lowered his own ambitions, he turned to the
humblest form of all, to his diary. During the surveyors' progress from the Great Dismal Swamp toward the Appalachians,

Byrd's diary automatically became a journal of their effort. Sometime in the subsequent ten years, he twice turned these journal notes into a history of the enterprise, each following the daily progress of the party as it went west. First came what is now called his *Secret History of the Line,* then the *History of the Dividing Line.* Largely uncirculated in his lifetime, these texts eventually established his reputation as a writer.[201] At the time, they established the dimensions of his maturity.

The idea that the expedition to run the dividing line could be the subject of a piece of literature dawned only slowly on Byrd in the months following the beginning of the expedition early in 1728. In his letters to Orrery and others in 1726 and 1727 he had already begun sketching in a powerful myth of the planter as pastoral patriarch, in order to justify his prudent "exile" to Virginia in terms he thought would be acceptable to members of the sophisticated world he had left behind in London. Yet at first his journey west into the swamps of the North Carolina border seemed to offer no further possibilities for extending this mythmaking process. After returning from the initial stage of the expedition, in the spring of 1728, Byrd apparently felt he was bankrupt of things to say. That summer he wrote to his wife's sister-in-law in England, Mrs. Jane Pratt Taylor, "My stars . . . [have] denyd me those smart qualitys [of invention] that might recommend me to [your] correspondence." "We can," he went on, only "pelt you with plaintive epistles." He said not a word to her of his recent journey along the border. But, after returning from the far more strenuous second stage of the survey late in 1728, Byrd had to write a long report to the Board of Trade. In this report he emphasized the hardships of the later stage of the journey, as the line was carried nearly to the mountains in the west. Perhaps he did this in order to justify his request for £400 in compensation, but the report to the Board of Trade seems to have sprung loose Byrd's fancy.[202]

Immediately thereafter, in April of 1729, he wrote again to

Jane Pratt Taylor, and by this time he was clearly aware that
running the line might have interesting dimensions. He tried
a cautious paragraph on her, as a possible entertainment.
"Since I had the pleasure of writeing to you I carryd the di-
videing line [on the second stage of the survey] betwixt this
country and Carolina quite up as high as the mountains. In
this journey we past thro the most charming country I ever
saw. Our dyet was venison, bear, and wild turkey, with all
which the woods supplyd us plentifully. Our drink indeed
was water but as pure as the waters of Paradise. . . . If the
people of England could but have a just notion of this fine
landskape, your island would quickly be dispeopled, and the
Parliament like that of Ireland, woud be forced to prohibit
people from transporting themselves out of their own country." In subsequent letters to more imposing correspondents
such as John Boyle, Baron Boyle of Broghill, Charles Boyle,
earl of Orrery, and John Perceval, Viscount Perceval, all written in the spring and early summer of 1729, Byrd began craft-
ing the mixture of entertainment and fable with which he
would ever after surround the running of the line.[203]

In the ensuing ten years, Byrd's discovery that a mundane
New World surveying party could be a vehicle for extending
in subtle ways his myth of himself-as-Virginian, and of Virginia as biblical paradise, would move from the realm of
letters into that of literary creation, and would emerge as two
full manuscript histories of the line. But at the same time,
these histories went far beyond the delicate protests of hard-
ship and the paeans of praise to the New World wilderness
with which Byrd so gratefully embellished his otherwise
newsless letters to his noble friends in England. Many of the
narrative techniques and eventual themes of the latter com-
positions were found only in embryo in his letters of 1729.
The ultimate histories of the dividing line which emerged in
the 1730s, the most fruitful period of William Byrd's life,
were more mature creations entirely.

It was a sign of great maturity that in the ultimate histories

Byrd took anything so humble as a daily journal as the genre
of his most sustained literary efforts. Gentlemen had long
kept travel journals, but journals were by definition relatively mundane affairs, as much record as art. Such common scribblers as Daniel Defoe had used the form at tedious
length and for profit.[204] But the new Byrd had a sense of context which enabled him to see that this was the appropriate
genre for his country. His letters to Orrery revealed that from
his return in 1726 he had been aware of the lessened role
high art must play in the New World.[205] At best the pastorale
rather than the more theatrical genres would be appropriate.
He was right. An epic about Virginia would inevitably have
become a mock epic. Even a mere pastorale might have been
pretentious. Besides, Byrd had set aside such artificial literary pretensions.[206] The humble journal was a more natural
form both for this country and for this man. But it must have
taken courage for Byrd to go from his private diary to a public
journal as he did in writing his two histories of the dividing
line. He was turning the genre of his most compulsive self
into what was clearly framed as a public essay. Essay, pastorale, satire, mock epic, and ultimately epic, one might add.
For Byrd the writer was to transform the metaphor of the
humble journal as freely as he did the metaphors of his
station.

The prose of the histories was impressively simple. It was
designed to communicate substance as well as style. The *Secret History* began:

> The Governor and Council of Virginia in the year 1727
> received an express order from His Majesty to appoint
> commissioners who, in conjunction with others to be
> named by the government of North Carolina, should run
> the line betwixt the two colonies. The rule these gentle-
> men were directed to go by was a paper of proposals for-
> merly agreed on between the two governors, at that time
> Spotswood and Eden.[207]

This tone reflected the fact that Byrd himself was now a person of substance, not just of style. He had been singled out from the Council to be trusted with the substantive matter at hand, and was now relating this matter in enlarged dimensions to the reader. The man had matured before the style but now, years after his anathemizing of wit, a useful style had emerged when he needed it. Both Byrd's choice of genre and his style, then, were the products of his maturity. In both a studied simplicity would convey volumes.

In both histories Byrd used these simple tools ultimately to transform a mundane episode into a minor epic of mastery. So much is new about the writer that one scarcely knows where to begin to delight in his powers. He relates the history of the previous controversies over the dividing line, calmly transports us to the border on the sea whence the true line will begin, and on the way west narrates the human fauna around him with an amused eye. He has entered and portrays engagingly the real world of human history. Only very slowly does the deepest burden of his performance emerge. Each history is to be an epic of the running of the line hidden within the modest form of a journal and disguised in a deprecating wit. Alongside this westward epic is the epic of William Byrd's natural mastery over those around him on their great journey.

In the *Secret History*, much of the mastery is the shared mastery of men over women. Byrd reveals that he never let a country wench go by without speculation on her sexual possibilities, which he plainly assumes any of the men might have appropriated had they attempted with a modicum of grace. But in Byrd's account he stops short of doing so because this is unbecoming in the leader of the dozens of woodsmen, assistants, surveyors, Carolina commissioners, and Virginia commissioners who make up the party. He does, after all, identify himself in this account as "Steddy." The opposite is the case with his rival Virginia commissioner, "Firebrand," who tries to seduce the daughter of one household while his equally unworthy servant imitates his example with her sister.

> Our landlord had not the good fortune to please Fire-brand with our dinner, but, surely, when people do their best, a reasonable man would be satisfied. But he en-deavored to mend his entertainment by making hot love to honest Ruth, who would by no means be charmed ei-ther with his persuasion or his person. While the master was employed in making love to one sister, the man made his passion known to the other; only he was more boisterous and employed force when he could not suc-ceed by fair means. Though one of the men rescued the poor girl from this violent lover but was so much his friend as to keep the shameful secret from those whose duty it would have been to punish such violations of hospitality. Nor was this the only one this disorderly fel-low was guilty of, for he broke open a house where our landlord kept the fodder for his own use, upon the belief that it was better than what he allowed us. This was in compliment to his master's horses, I hope, and not in blind obedience to any order he received from him.[208]

Firebrand emerges as the antithesis of Byrd's new "Steddy" model of himself as a gentleman. Steddy is sexually re-strained while Firebrand is nearly a rapist. Firebrand is "ar-rogant" while Steddy is humble: "This being my birthday, I adored the goodness of Heaven for having indulged me with so much health and very uncommon happiness in the course of fifty-four years, in which my sins have been many and my sufferings few, my opportunities great but my improve-ments small." Steddy ministers to the men when they are ill, Firebrand does not. Firebrand, indeed, abuses the men. He ex-presses the belief that in all disputes with the men "a gentle-man should be believed on his bare word without evidence and a poor man condemned without trial." "Which," con-tinues Steddy, "agreed not at all with my notions of justice."[209] Firebrand's worst sin is to aspire to the leadership of the party and to enlist in his cause the clownish commissioners from North Carolina. Steddy opposes to this presumption a cheerful patience in the face of all obstacles. Steddy's patience, with the just support of Governor Gooch when Firebrand becomes insufferable, brings the Virginia surveyors nearly to the mountains long after Firebrand and his Carolina friends have given up the quest.[210]

The *Secret History of the Line* has its faults. It is obsessed with sex. It is at times gossipy, waspish, and even nasty as Byrd takes out his hostility on Firebrand in the relative heat of the years immediately after the event. It is as if Byrd had to struggle to exorcise his former brittle, ambitious self as he encountered it in the person of Firebrand. But the history is a lucid narrative of a tense political situation in the midst of a dangerous journey through a wilderness inhabited by hostile Indians. It is usually gentle in featuring its writer as the mature gentleman who brings the epic journey to a successful conclusion.

In this respect, it is not so much Virginia's Firebrand who is the antitype of Steddy as it is the clownish commissioners of North Carolina. With their hangers-on, these Falstaffs, Malvolios, and Sir Toby Belches populate the thickets of the borderline in hilarious parody of William Byrd's, and Virginia's, newfound maturity.

20 [March]. No news yet of our Dismalites [the actual surveyors, now crossing the Dismal Swamp], though we dispatched men to every point of the compass to inquire after them. Our visitors took their leave, but others came in the evening to supply their places. Judge Jumble [a Carolina commissioner], who left us at Currituck, returned now from Edenton and brought three cormorants along with him. One was his own brother, the second was brother to Shoebrush [another Carolina commissioner], and the third, Captain Genneau, who had sold

his commission and spent the money. These honest gentlemen had no business but to help drink out our liquor, having very little at home. Shoebrush's brother is a collector and owes his place to a bargain he made with Firebrand. Never were understrappers so humble as the North Carolina collectors are to this huge man. They pay him the same colirt they would do if they held their commissions immediately from his will and pleasure, though the case is much otherwise, because their commissions are as good as his, being granted by the same commissioners of His Majesty's Customs. However, he expects a world of homage from them, calling them his officers. Nor is he content with homage only, but he taxes them, as indeed he does all the other collectors of his province, with a hundred little services.

At night the noble captain retired before the rest of the company and was stepping without ceremony into our bed, but I arrived just time enough to prevent it. We could not possibly be so civil to this free gentleman as to make him so great a compliment, much less let him take possession, according to the Carolina breeding, without invitation. Had Ruth or Rachel, my landlord's daughters, taken this liberty, we should perhaps have made no words, but in truth the captain had no charms that merited so particular an indulgence.[211]

"Ah, well," Byrd seems to be saying, "one doesn't have to be much of a gentleman to show the way to this company!" In this way he showed that the perspective on himself, the ability to distance himself from himself, which he had once demonstrated in a far more mannered fashion in "Inamorato L'Oiseaux," was now complete. When he laughed at the clowns from North Carolina he laughed as well at himself. Byrd's *Secret History* is ultimately a modest, and almost a self-mocking, celebration of the Virginia "breeding" he had decided to accept.

But the *Secret History* was also a measure of the paradoxical dimensions of Byrd's maturity, as he could never bring
himself to publish it. He did not even circulate it privately.
Its lascivious eye and the sometimes gossipy account of
Steddy's rivalry with Firebrand seemed unbecoming to Byrd.
So perhaps did its very modesty. So he imposed a kind of creative censorship on it by transmuting it into a new version.
Sometime in the 1730s, reaching for a greater dignity than
the *Secret History* could afford, he created the longer *History
of the Dividing Line*.[212] The sex and gossip were almost entirely absent. What took their place was the studied pose of
a natural historian in the New World. Plants, and erudite
knowledge, grew profusely in the spaces where scandal had
grown before.

> We observed abundance of coltsfoot and maidenhair in
> many places and nowhere a larger quantity than here.
> They are both excellent pectoral plants and seem to have
> greater virtues much in this part of the world than in
> more northern climates; and I believe it may pass for a
> rule in botanics that where any vegetable is planted by
> the hand of Nature it has more virtue than in places
> whereto it is transplanted by the curiosity of man. . . .

> They [the surveyors] returned by the path they had made
> in coming out and with great industry arrived in the eve-
> ning at the spot where the line had been discontinued.
> After so long and laborious a journey, they were glad to
> repose themselves on their couches of cypress bark,
> where their sleep was as sweet as it would have been on
> a bed of Finland down.

> In the meantime, we who stayed behind had nothing to
> do but to make the best observations we could upon that
> part of the country. The soil of our landlord's plantation,
> though none of the best, seemed more fertile than any
> thereabouts, where the ground is near as sandy as the

deserts of Africa and consequently barren. The road leading from thence to Edenton, being in distance about twenty-seven miles, lies upon a ridge called Sandy Ridge, which is so wretchedly poor that it will not bring potatoes. The pines in this part of the country are of a different species from those that grow in Virginia: their bearded leaves are much longer and their cones much larger. Each cell contains a seed of the size and figure of a black-eyed pea, which, shedding in November, is very good mast for hogs and fattens them in a short time.[213]

The hero of the *History of the Dividing Line* is in this guise more pretentious than his predecessor in the *Secret History*. From the manager of an irritating rivalry Byrd becomes the scientific observer still farther above the crowd. But in compensation this more dignified Byrd drops the name "Steddy" to become simply "I" and all the other characters regain their true names. The prose style remains simple and the story is still a fascinating epic. By its very length this version conveys the exhaustion of the remaining members of the original party as they emerge at last from the hilly thickets grasping a map of the border as their prize. The friendship of these survivors regardless of rank is conveyed by Byrd's use of "we" at the end to describe the party, by his gratitude for their good health, and by his giving a "full share of credit" to his "brave fellows" for the service "we performed."[214] As these woodsmen disperse to their homes, it becomes clear that a gentle epic suitable to the New World has been created out of William Byrd's journal.

More, in the *History of the Dividing Line* Byrd suddenly articulated all that had bothered him about North Carolina. In an uncharacteristic outburst which had its origins in the bumpkins satirized in the *Secret History*, but which went far beyond them to the true source of Byrd's irritation with the feckless frontier society along the border, Byrd emitted his famous portrait of "lubberland."

Both cattle and hogs ramble into the neighboring marshes and swamps, where they maintain themselves the whole winter long and are not fetched home till the spring. Thus these indolent wretches during one half of the year lose the advantage of the milk of their cattle, as well as their dung, and many of the poor creatures perish in the mire, into the bargain, by this ill management. Some who pique themselves more upon industry than their neighbors will now and then, in compliment to their cattle, cut down a tree whose limbs are loaded with moss afore-mentioned. The trouble would be too great to climb the tree in order to gather this provender, but the shortest way (which in this country is always counted the best) is to fell it, just like the lazy Indians.

The only business here is raising of hogs, which is managed with the least trouble and affords the diet they are most fond of. The truth of it is, the inhabitants of North Carolina devour so much swine's flesh that it fills them full of gross humors. [This results in] yaws, [which first] seizes the throat, next the palate, and lastly shows its spite to the poor nose, of which 'tis apt in a small time treacherously to undermine the foundation. . . . Surely there is no place in the world where the inhabitants live with less labor than in North Carolina. It approaches nearer to the description of Lubberland than any other, by the great felicity of the climate, the easiness of raising provisions, and the slothfulness of the people. . . .

I believe this [Edenton, N.C.] is the only metropolis in the Christian or Mahometan world where there is neither church, chapel, mosque, synagogue, or any other place of public worship of any sect or religion whatsoever. . . . They account it among their greatest advantages that they are not priest-ridden, not remembering that the clergy is rarely guilty of bestriding such as have the misfortune to be poor. One thing [which] may be said for the inhabitants of [this] province, [is] that they are not troubled with any religious fumes. . . . What little devotion there may happen to be is much more private than their vices.

A citizen here is counted extravagant if he has ambition enough to aspire to a brick chimney. Justice herself is but indifferently lodged, the courthouse having much of the air of a common tobacco house. . . . They are rarely guilty of flattering or making any court to their governors but treat them with all the excesses of freedom and familiarity. They are of opinion their rulers would be apt to grow insolent if they grew rich, and for that reason take care to keep them poorer and more dependent, if possible, than the saints in New England used to do their governors. . . . Another reason . . . the government there is so loose and the laws so feebly executed [is] that . . . everyone does just what seems good in his own eyes. If the governor's hands have been weak in that province, . . . much weaker, then, were the hands of the magistrate, who, though he might have had virtue enough to endeavor to punish offenders, which very rarely happened, [found himself] quite impotent for want of ability to put it in execution. . . . [One] bold magistrate, . . . taking upon him to order a fellow to the stocks for being disorderly in his drink, was for his intemperate zeal carried thither himself and narrowly escaped being whipped by the rabble into the bargain.[215]

Byrd here reveals the central shock of his experiences running the dividing line, namely his encounter with the rude English and Scots-Irish settlers of "lubberland." Reading between the lines, one can see his fear of a "lazy" society where gentlemen such as himself were neither needed nor respected. It seems to have sent a shiver up William Byrd's spine to contemplate a future America in which such crude democracy might erode the civilizing influence only now achieved by the gentry in Virginia. All their schooling, all their hard-won maturity would, together with his own achievement in joining them as a constructive member, be washed away in a sea of social barbarism to the southwest. These Virginia gentlemen would have risen safely above the challenging rabble of Bacon's Rebellion only to be undermined by the insolence of a growing western rabble a generation or two later.

But Byrd's reaction to the "lubberland" on the borders had never been passive. When he had returned from actually running the line in 1728 he had taken two vital steps to prevent that future which could be seen developing to the west. He had ordered his father's old ramshackle manse at Westover, much added on to in the nearly fifty years since it was first occupied, to be replaced by an imposing brick mansion house. Rising in red brick, with two stories and a lofty attic, on the rising landscape facing the James River, the main structure of the new "Westover" was probably as close to an English manor house as any Virginia manse of the early eighteenth century. It was also one of the first of the new manor houses of the golden age of the Virginia gentry. Lest it be thought that the message of social deference given by this new "Westover" was accidental, Byrd simultaneously acquired more than 100,000 acres immediately west of "lubberland." For years, he sacrificed immediate returns from these grants while trying to enlist orderly German-speaking Swiss settlers for his western acres. In his pamphlet written to attract the German-Swiss, he rejected the Scots-Irish who then predominated in the backcountry by saying that he wanted no "mixed people from Pennsylvania," whom he regarded as "like the Goths and Vandals of old." One glimpse of lubberland had been enough for him. But William Byrd had no crippling fear of lubberland either, for it was also just after the actual running of the line that he gave up his rooms in London, symbolically committing himself to Virginia's future.[216]

A vision of great English manors presiding over far-flung

villages of deferential German-Swiss had, then, been Byrd's immediate antidote to what he had seen in 1728, one he worked years to realize. It was a powerfully creative vision of an alternative America which the narcissistic young planter of 1709 could never have obtained, let alone worked long to realize. That narcissist had scarcely had a horizon beyond his next letter in pursuit of a higher office. The mature Byrd had given up his rooms in England and had worked systematically to realize his alternative to social chaos. He was to abandon the essential part of it only in 1739 when a ship carrying German-Swiss settlers foundered in Lynnhaven Bay, drowning with the settlers his mature dreams.[217]

But Byrd had begun one further enterprise in the years immediately after returning from running the line in 1728, one which had perhaps been a final part of his plan to buttress the forces of order in America. Sometime after 1729 but before 1735 he had begun writing the first of his histories of the dividing line.[218] In this perspective, these emerging literary efforts may have been part of an effort to affirm not only Byrd's, but also the Virginia gentry's importance in civilizing the wilderness. "Steddy," by whatever name he went, was a gentleman who was representative of a class of men which alone could direct the running of coherent lines through an incoherent wilderness. As such he was less pretentious than his English equivalents, but far more necessary. The line this leader ran was, ultimately, a social line. On one side was a social order, emanating in its essence from men like himself. On the other, was the social chaos of lubberland. In this perspective William Byrd's two histories of the dividing line were brilliant acts of creativity. They were the arguments for the hierarchical society he sought to buttress. What they said was that in the New World men could choose between running like hogs through the limitless woods, or serving under a man they loved, to draw the lines which guided them all. Properly understood, Byrd's histories are astonishing feats. A man who had lived outside history now sought to remake it with every resource at his disposal, as a long-term actor in that history. His bricks and mortar, his land, and his highest literary skills were at the service of a vision of history remade.[219] He was flexing the greatest metaphor of all.

It is odd how far Byrd had come by the time he finished the *History of the Dividing Line* in the mid-1730s. From Elyot's *Boke Called the Governour* he had learned as one of many rote precepts to read in Lucian and Homer. So he had bought their works twice over and had read in them more than in all other authors combined. Like Lucian of Samosata himself, Byrd had at times been no more than a provincial satirist. He had stood implicitly in the Attic purity of colonial status and, in many of his portraits and poems, satirized the foibles of London, the English Rome. Then in "The Female Creed," also like Lucian, he had matured into compassionate satire not dependent on poking fun at the imperial center.[220] Finally, in the histories he had gone beyond Lucian to pose his Attic Virginia as a purer Rome, which itself must be buttressed against barbarians to the west. His fortunes and his eloquence now went to this end.

Yet not his eloquence. For in the end our William Byrd was still the old William Byrd of "Inamorato L'Oiseaux." Fearing rejection, he could not publish even the more dignified *History of the Dividing Line.* He lent it to the naturalist Peter Collinson in 1736, with the strict stipulation that it not be spread about. It was not ready to publish, Byrd said, in a terrible echo of his frightened youth, because it still needed "a decent skin drawn over all to keep things tight in their places, and prevent their looking frightfull."[221] He still could not bear for his feelings to be seen. Byrd never found a literary skin thick enough to hold himself in and thin enough to see through. Childhood haunts us all; it cost Byrd his highest achievement. The histories never did what they may have been intended to do, reaffirm publicly a Virginia gentry which was indeed in danger of losing its newfound grip. Nor could

Byrd ever receive recognition for the grace of his affirmation.

Ironically it would be Edmund Ruffin who would finally publish the *History of the Dividing Line* more than one hundred years later, in 1841. Ruffin was all his life preoccupied with the increasingly sterile soil and sterile culture of nineteenth-century tidewater Virginia. Perhaps he saw Byrd's *History* as a reflection of a time when the tidewater gentry was still optimistic about its capability to set the lines for society. If so, the *History* was only a temporary bulwark against Ruffin's own version of his culture's final despair. In 1865 when the South lost the Civil War, Ruffin committed suicide. Byrd's son, plagued by his own debts rather than his father's, had committed suicide ninety years before.[222] Over the intervening years many of the tidewater gentry would lie down in darkness. Others would be absorbed in more modern lubberlands.

Whether it would have done any good or not, because of his final block Byrd's *History* went unpublished in his time, and his political maturity had to confine itself to Virginia politics for its public expression. Through the later 1730s he continued the general struggle against the London merchants, probably occupied his new house "Westover," and for a time longer persisted in his efforts to obtain German-Swiss for the "Land of Eden" he wanted to create in the Roanoke area.[223] In still another unpublished journal, *A Progress to the Mines in the Year 1732*, he revealed that he had at last been reconciled with his old enemy Alexander Spotswood. Like Byrd, Spotswood had become a Virginian. Like Byrd he was determined to civilize the west and saw German culture as part of the solution. In 1732, Byrd had visited Spotswood at Germanna, his new home in the west. The two old men, both now in their late fifties, walked together in the gardens. They compared notes on their industrious efforts in the manufacture of iron. They talked politics, as old rivals will.

Spotswood, like Byrd, was by now a convinced defender of American liberties. He told Byrd he did not see how Parliament could ever tax Americans without exciting a righteous opposition which the British could not quell. They parted friends. A few years later, when Spotswood died in military service to the crown, Byrd led the effort to get a pension for his widow.[224]

Byrd's letters had eased in tone through the years to match first his maturity and then his age. The vigorous displays of erudition with which he had sought, as recently as the late 1720s, to impress his well-placed friends in England gave way in the 1730s to nostalgic exchanges very like his final conversation with Spotswood. Ned Southwell's family had by now "drop't" Byrd, but the earl of Orrery, Sir Charles Wager, and others continued to respond. Mellow reflections on imperial strategy in the Caribbean supplemented reminiscences as Byrd still sought to impress friends such as Wager, highly placed in the military establishment, but it all had a gentle air.[225] Byrd's observations were sensible. He had nothing to gain.

Which left the diary. The diary of 1739–1741 is a document of Byrd's old age. He was sixty-five when it began, sixty-seven when it ended.[226] He would die three years later. By this time maturity had shaded so far into old age that they had become indistinguishable. He had been a Virginian for only thirteen years, or ten, if giving up his rooms in London in 1729 had been the sign of his final commitment. He had finished the histories not long before. He would publish neither. His debts, though not his old ambition, had driven him to make a last inquiry about a governorship at about the same time. The German-Swiss settlers had just foundered on the cold American shore. Byrd had matured late and never completely. Once matured, fate had not been wholly on his side. Now the last limitations on him were being put by the biology that limits all persons. He accepted these in turn, but with calm rather than apathy. This is the mood of the late diary.

13 [March 1741]. I rose about 6, read Hebrew and Greek. I prayed and had hominy. I danced. The weather was cold and cloudy with some rain and thunder, the wind southwest. I settled accounts and walked about the plantation till dinner when I ate cold mutton. Jenny was a little better, thank God. I wrote English till the evening and then walked again. At night read English and prayed. My cold continued. It rained.

14. I rose about 6, read Hebrew and Greek. I prayed and had tea. I danced. The weather was clear and warm, the wind southwest. Jenny was a little better, thank God. I read English and walked. About one came Mr. Fontaine [the parson] to dinner and I ate neat's tongue. After dinner we talked and walked about the plantation. I talked with my people and prayed.

15. I rose about 6, read Hebrew and Greek. I prayed and had coffee. I danced. The weather was cold and clear, the wind north. About 11 I went to church and had a learned sermon. After dinner Mrs. Carter, John Stith and his wife, Colonel Eppes and his son Ned, and Captain Dunlop dined with us and I ate boiled beef. After dinner we talked and had coffee. Most of the company went away but Mrs. Carter, Jenny Anderson, John Stith and his wife stayed. I talked with my people.

16. I rose about 6, read Hebrew and Greek. I prayed and had coffee. I danced. The weather was cold and cloudy, the wind southeast. Beside our company Johnny Ravenscroft and Mr. Miller came to dine with us. We played cards till dinner. I ate roast rabbit. After dinner we talked and had coffee, and our company went away. I talked with my people and prayed.

17. I rose about 6, read Hebrew and Greek. I prayed and had coffee. I danced. The weather was cold and cloudy, the wind north. I sent up the boat with a good wind and

about 11 went to visit Beverley Randolph but he was
from home so we proceeded to Dick Randolph's, where
we found Parson Stith, and I ate tripe. After dinner we
took leave and the coach stuck about two miles from
home so that we sent for our horses and got well home at
last and found all well, thank God.

18.   I rose about 6, read Hebrew and Greek. I prayed and
had tea. I danced. The weather was warm and cloudy,
with rain sometimes, the wind south. Mrs. Harrison
sent some fish which we had for dinner. In the afternoon
it thundered and blew hard but held up time enough for
us to walk in the garden. At night I talked with my
people and prayed.

The mornings still belonged to the boy who had encoded
his personality in routines later written by a young man into
a secret diary. William Byrd still read Hebrew and Greek. He
still prayed, and ate one dish per meal. When he was not infirm he still "danced." When he had been sick and was well
again he "danced" every day to make up for lost time. He still
rehearsed these routines after the fact in a diary probably
written every morning in the same shorthand code. The old
personality was not entirely gone. It had kept him from publishing his histories and it would keep him at his secret diary
until near his death. But Byrd was no longer the same man.
These remnants of the behavioral routine, like their continuing secret rehearsal in the diary, seem simply to have been a
calm prelude to days which were superficially similar to but
in essence deeply different from the days of the young Virginia planter. What remained of his routine was simply a
touchstone by which Byrd linked his past to a transformed
present. Once this stone was touched, he went on to other
things. Great chunks of the rest of his solitary routine had
long since been permanently abridged or discarded. "Danced
my dance" had become merely "danced." The bout of Latin
each morning, sometimes followed by more Greek, was long

gone. Perhaps he still did his accounts and "arranged" himself at midmorning, but it was no longer necessary to study these things in the diary if he did. As he moved out into the world, probably earlier in the day now than before, he may still have exercised emotional balance, moderation, and restraint, but he had long ago stopped studying his own composure in the secret diary. Even more than he had already begun to be in 1720, in the middle diary, he was now free for other things.

Virginia life had not changed, but he had. There were still overseers to manage, for Byrd had always managed people rather than plantations. There was business to do and people to see. Yet the compulsive visiting of his youth, and of his middle life in London and in Virginia, was now over. Old men did not need to pursue "acquaintance." Old men could please themselves. The people Byrd did see were far less often the objects of little vignettes of mastery. Scarcely at all. They were friends. What they did was "talk," and "talk," and "talk." They talked to one another, enjoying being the subjects of one another's affections, as old friends do. Such at any rate is the tone of the late diary. There were few friends, usually the parson or near neighbors. Byrd's wife is seldom mentioned save to evoke his concern when she is ill, but time and again she was included in the relaxed "we" Byrd now used so frequently to describe those closest to him. He knew that she was there. In some ways it was a sparse life, with less business, fewer visits, and no quarrels with his wife. But it was a world of long, affectionate conversations with friends. "After dinner we talked of many things."[227] Maturity had come in time to give Byrd a warm old age.

Politics was still present, but was by now also a calm, natural part of Byrd's life. His family still concerned him. His son and daughters occasionally flitted across the scene bringing friends to visit, or not, studying their lessons under their father's supervision, playing billiards with him. On January 16, 1741, "This was my daughter Mary's [fourteenth] birthday;

God preserve her many happy years." As he had with Lucy, he occasionally dreamed that Maria had died. He once dreamed that he would die.[228] But in general death was a far less threatening specter than it had been to the brittle young man in his thirties. Death evoked not so much fear as a resigned compassion in this older man. "I had bad dreams and thought I should die in a short time, but as for that, God's will be done." On a January night, "It snowed again. God save dumb creatures."[229] Never were the silences between his few words more eloquent than in this late diary.

His relations with his slaves grew more intimate though also more paradoxical. Make no mistake, the overseers on Byrd's other plantations went on whipping their slaves. Even at Westover, to have the friendship of the master was still slavery. But at Westover there had been a transformation. Begun in 1720 and 1721, it was now complete. Whippings had become virtually nonexistent. Contractual agreements between master and slave had somewhat taken their place.[230] The paradox was that so had sexual relations. One admires but mostly agonizes over a sixty-seven-year-old man, who had long avoided sexual play with his female slaves as a matter of pride, now reduced to "playing the fool with Sally."[231] The most moving sign of Byrd's need for comfort was not in his relationship with Sally, however; it was in the way he ended most days with the now deeply established ritual, "I talked with my people and prayed."[232] A master who insisted nightly that he had "good health, good thoughts, and good humor, thanks be to God Almighty" was surely less bearable than one who "talked with my people and prayed." What comfort he or the slaves found in this is not known.

For the older William Byrd, life had become a reciprocal conversation with his friends. On different terms, it had become a reciprocal conversation with his slaves. The last diary's entries are short and their tone is calm because the diary has been superseded by conversations. Shortly before his death, Byrd lived almost entirely in the real world. The diary was a companion from his past to which he confided, as to another old friend, his mellower existence. Frantic precept had become calm metaphor. The genre contained in these little books had made a long journey.

Byrd's last year was marked by two symbolic victories. By 1744 Micajah Perry the younger had had to declare the firm of Perry and Lane bankrupt. The Virginia planters had retaliated against his leadership of the London merchants' campaign to confiscate their estates for debt, something these merchants never quite got to do, by denying him their business. In the midst of this near boycott, Byrd had taken the heroic step of actually selling land and slaves and so had essentially paid off his debts to Perry even as he had reduced his business to help drive Perry bankrupt. In the end he was solvent while Perry had gone under. In 1743, James Blair had died at the age of eighty-seven, leaving vacant the presidency of the Council of Virginia. Byrd, next in seniority on the Council, became Blair's successor.[233] For the rest of 1743 and for as long as he lived in 1744, William Byrd occupied this, the second highest office in Virginia. Had Governor Gooch been absent during these months, Byrd would have been acting governor. At the age of sixty-nine William Byrd had finally reached the highest place ever occupied by his father.

XII

Stories such as William Byrd's demonstrate what T. S. Eliot called "the intersection of the timeless with time." The timeless is the universal question of youth, upbringing, and experience, of maturity or the failure to mature. Time decides the context in which these events take place. To relate the universal process of personal growth in any given time, to let these two intersect, is to understand a little of the nature of that particular time in which the process occurred. The story of the intersection of the timeless universals of an individual life within the special context of a historical time is often very moving. That with which we can identify in ourselves is always blended with the effort to explain a time which is irretrievably different. Such is the wonder of any historical narrative.

William Byrd's particular story will have to be told differently than it has been here. There is so much information published, so much still in the archives, so much of it cryptic or undated, so much open to interpretation, that it is a story which could be retold endlessly. The point of this essay is only to say that it should be retold, endlessly, as it is an especially moving story of the intersection of the timeless with a time we little understand. Byrd's time in particular, early eighteenth-century Virginia, is a time Americans will always reach for in some lost historical consciousness, as if it is a story we once knew but cannot quite remember. That is why our historians debate so over it. It is a time so mythic that it convinces us we have real memories of it, and it will be debated because people will always argue fiercely over whose memory is the right one. Such tribal arguments over tribal memory should never stop.

Having come so far, one does not really want to say more, but only to pass the torch to those who will remember William Byrd differently. The universal element of the story makes one want to leave Byrd in peace for now after whatever long journey, perhaps a bit like the one described here, he made. Leave him in peace, he is like me, his story seems to say, even though he is in fact not like this author at all. Leave him in peace whatever his odyssey. His was the epic of a man who was not an epic man. Yet the hints of a way of seeing biography, and history, which lie in this version of his story, and the hints of the nature of William Byrd's own time in history, call for a little reflection at the end.

What is remarkable, first of all, is the way personality and genre, life and text, interacted through time in Byrd's life. Bacon's Rebellion, and a reaching for gentry culture, shaped a personality which expressed itself in all its pathology and charm in the genres available to it within the culture of the eighteenth-century English gentleman. Further events created the conditions under which that personality would alter itself from within, so to speak, reaching a maturity that produced constructive political action as well as a mature literary genre within Virginia. While such developments are revealing of the nature of "maturity" as it arrived within one personality, they do not significantly extend psychological definitions of maturity save insofar as they point outward, to that personality's relationship with its culture. Events, personality, and genre were followed by new events, by an altered personality, and by a new genre. It is an intricate, revealing perspective on the historical process which looks within and yet beyond the individual.

What that perspective captures initially is an inside view of the process of enculturation. Culture may have been a cage for William Byrd, but it was a large and flexible cage within which he eventually learned to fly. He learned to transform freely the metaphors of that culture, even though in the end his culture-produced personality and sheer time clipped his wings a bit. But in this perspective it is unfair to speak of culture as a cage. Culture was restricting only so long as it *was* precept, and, as precept, created and reinforced a rigidly pathological strain in Byrd's personality. Culture also offered him, and helped by circumstances he accepted, a version of itself as metaphor. Culture as metaphor was not at all a cage.[234] It was the possibility of flight, the wings, the air in which one could fly. When Byrd could flex his view of the gentleman's role enough to flatter a burgess, to be openly grateful for neighborly affection, and simply to go out and talk with his slaves, when in the process of preserving a political culture in which he had become an adaptable, constructive actor he could turn a humble diary into a simple journal and a simple journal into an unexpected epic of the need for steady, cheerful gentlemen to run the lines of order through the chaos of the wilderness, and when by this he could clearly mean lines of social order through a social wilderness as well, then William Byrd was flexing the metaphors of his class within the Virginia version of eighteenth-century gentry culture. Flexed, these metaphors became liberating. Then culture was limiting only in that diffuse sense in which all cultures are limiting. They define the conscious and unconscious terms in which we live.

Within these larger limits culture offered William Byrd a vast sphere of possibilities. Like any culture, it offered him the choice of pathological immaturity if he persisted in regarding his roles within that culture as precepts compulsively to be repeated. Fortunately, his childhood, lonely as it seems to have been and devoid of close mentors who could explain how to flex the metaphors available to him, was still not so devoid of possibilities that he was doomed to the pathology of a preceptual relationship with his culture. To watch Byrd learn instead to flex what were in fact not precepts but metaphors is to sense the range of the possibilities which any culture offers. If culture was at first Byrd's cage it was also to become the medium of a most remarkable flight.

Culture was, to use another term, the medium of his maturity.[235] Byrd's pathological side and his substantial recovery from it teach us to define maturity in cultural terms. Only by studying someone who has missed the point of his culture and become locked into a preceptual relationship with it, is it possible fully to appreciate the great mobility of the relationship between a healthy individual and his culture. Culture is, in a sense, created in the ongoing use of metaphors by healthy individuals. Such persons need not be rich, as Byrd was. Ordinary individuals can have such a relationship with their cultures as well. Most usually do. William Gooch senior of Brockdish, Norfolk, England, no relation to the Virginia governor of the same name but rather only a plain barber, was such a man a generation later. So, if current studies are right, were even slaves on Virginian plantations, though they were far more constrained by circumstance.[236] As it was with them, so, between 1720 and 1744, was it with William Byrd II of Westover.

Byrd's ultimate limits as he matured within this culture were set not so much by his culture as by the residue of a pathological personality created at an earlier cultural moment and by milder circumstance. But limits are felt in proportion to resources, so Byrd may have felt these limits keenly. He had taken English gentry culture to its limits by transforming fears of the Scots-Irish into a massive plan to settle German-Swiss settlers to the west of lubberland as a guarantee of a deferential society even there. He had stretched English gentry culture as it was known in Virginia beyond its old limits by finding in the journal of a wilderness surveying party the subtle epic which would express the virtue of cheerful gentlemen amidst the potential democratic chaos of America. But his personality had hidden his cleverly disguised epic in a skin so tight that no one saw it for generations after he died, and fate had finally wrecked his German-Swiss settlers at Lynnhaven Bay. His present culture was not to blame, but it must have been frustrating.

The relationship of personality to genre has been perhaps the central illuminator of the relationship between the individual and culture as seen from Byrd's perspective. In Byrd's case at least, personality encountered its culture very often in the form not of interactions with other individuals—though these were clearly involved as well—but in the form of the available literary genres. In his case, though there are exceptions both early and late in his life, the distinction between a compulsively preceptual use of nearly all available genres (letters partially excepted) early in life and a flexible, "metaphorical" use of new genres late in life is very striking. There is more to be explored in this insight about a maturity so lucent in Byrd's development as a writer. The "old criticism" of texts as historical creations may have much to teach historical anthropologists about the inner and outer limits for individuals of that realm of expression loosely known as culture. Having no living tribes, most historical anthropologists must use such texts as those which, in Byrd's life, give so much of the dynamic of his enculturation. Further, the eloquence of Byrd's laconic diary with respect to enculturation is particularly helpful in moving the study of diaries out from the shadow of the verbose Samuel Pepys.[237]

Byrd's life establishes more than the scope of culture and definitions of cultural maturity within it. It sets up a commentary on the nature of cultural change. For from another perspective, any life of William Byrd is a fascinating study in the construction of the Virginia variant of the wider gentry culture of eighteenth-century Anglo-America. It catches Byrd's father reaching for the original. It catches the long process by which William Byrd II finally adapted this original to local circumstance in order to maintain something like the cultural hegemony this class-culture enjoyed in the British Isles at the time. Culture being borrowed in this way is something anthropologists seldom catch. If they capture any dynamic, it is usually the impending destruction of native cultures by modernity. What the life of William Byrd shows in this respect may be something a bit different. It may show the terrible costs provincials could pay to reach for and ultimately to adapt the mother culture in their own context.

Here three cases stand in point. One is William Byrd as presented here. Another is Landon Carter, as seen by Rhys Isaac.[238] The last is Robert Carter, in the view of Shomer Zwelling.[239] Byrd was born in 1674 and died in 1744. Landon Carter, born in 1710 and died in 1778, was the uncle of Robert Carter, who was born in 1728 and died in 1804. The two Carters might be described as members of the second or even of the third generation of great Virginia planters. Byrd and

Landon Carter were both sent to England as youths for a gentleman's education. The greatest pressure was on Byrd as a member of that generation educated immediately after Bacon's Rebellion. He was faced with becoming an alternative to the chaos of that event. But Virginia gentry culture was never perfectly secure, as Byrd's later portrait of lubberland reveals. At about the time Byrd was reacting in shock to his experiences of frontier democracy after running the line, Landon Carter was sent away to school in England, possibly for related reasons. For in Virginia the image of a perfect English gentry had constantly to be reasserted before the eyes of a skeptical audience.[240] Moreover, real advancement within or outside of Virginia might still depend on such genteel perfections as could be found in an English education. Given the planters' mounting debts after 1725, such advancement might be the key to financial solvency. So might the legal knowledge they acquired in England. So Landon Carter as well was sent away.

Both Byrd and Carter were sent away as boys to borrow the perfections of English gentry culture so as to be better able to maintain order in a context where aristocracy as a principle was constantly threatened. That principle was threatened by ridicule of their recent ancestry both by their fellow settlers and by their English governors, by frontier skepticism such as that encountered in lubberland, by the embarrassment of debt, by lack of legal knowledge, and eventually, by the leveling ideology of evangelical religion. Some fathers reacted by concluding that the perfect model of the English gentry had constantly to be renewed from England, and these two boys and others like them bore that terrible burden. They bore it alone, for crossing the Atlantic was a dangerous two-month voyage. Their parents did not see them again for years. Because ships sailed only irregularly, letters came at intervals of many months. For all of them who were sent abroad in this way, it was an exile to a land where what was left them of their families was their responsibility to come home perfect gentlemen. Yet their colonial status only guaranteed them further rejections in England.[241]

If these two men are any example, it was nearly a crippling legacy. William Byrd froze under the twin burdens of responsibility and rejection. He tried to do everything expected of him and so became a parody of the culture he had been sent to acquire. He was also deeply ambivalent about the mother culture and about its Virginia variant. Having been rejected by both, he could not find his cultural home in either. His compulsive behavior ensured that this would remain so for a long time to come. He was for this reason unsuccessful in mastering the complex Virginia environment on his first return there. Only after nearly a decade of purgatory did he emerge by a near miracle into a healthy relationship in Virginia with the role assigned him to perfect so long before. Then he adapted that role brilliantly to Virginia's needs as he finally saw these. He wrote an epic for a country which needed yet could not easily sustain an epic. But he was too timid to publish it. His maturity had its limits. Landon Carter was also deeply ambivalent about the role awaiting him back in Virginia. He never felt comfortable in it, as he could not stand public scrutiny of his imperfections. He was known as a hypersensitive man. Carter found his way out by extending the role of the perfect-English-gentleman-turned-planter-in-Virginia into realms not previously considered by other gentleman planters. Rigidly, he mastered the rules of order as no one yet had, and so gained an unexpected if short-lived status in the House of Burgesses. More flexibly, he adapted the new English model of the gentleman as enlightened agriculturalist, creating a subrole which was to become a part of the model for all gentlemen in Virginia as well. Because he was nearly the first in this role, Landon Carter could feel secure from public scrutiny.

Clearly, both William Byrd and Landon Carter felt too vulnerable to bear the terrible cultural burden placed upon them as boys. Both broke down in different ways in their pressured roles as adapters of a foreign model of perfection in a new context. Byrd tried too hard. Carter was uncomfortable. Both struggled to reach a healthy way of acquitting their responsibilities to their families and to a society in need of an ordering principle. If Byrd and Carter were at all typical, provincial borrowing exacted a heavy price in human stress and in delayed maturity. It did so in the very men it most needed to be "perfect." There was something contradictory about the whole process. The resultant brittleness of the Virginia gentry may explain why they continued to be, or to feel, threatened, and why their response to the threat was sometimes only to pursue ever more feverishly that model of perfection which made such men as William Byrd and Landon Carter brittle for much of their lives. It seemed the contradictions would have no end.

Establishing a college, William and Mary, did not necessarily solve the cultural dilemma Virginians faced. Robert Carter, Landon's nephew, received a gentleman's education there from the age of nine, when he was sent there by his family in Gloucester County. But the tutors were usually English and the model all the more intensely English for being transplanted to Virginia. Full of the same ambivalence about his responsibilities and about his true home, Robert Carter ran away to England as soon as his father's estate and role in Virginia descended on him. The responsibility was too much and the true place for a gentleman, where he could be at ease in the natural home of that ideal, was too obvious. But perhaps Robert Carter was not really at home there either. Two years later, he returned to Virginia to a role and a duty he could scarcely bear. He twisted in agony to evade it throughout much of his adult life. He left politics, hid out in his house, became neurasthenically ill. As Byrd was apparently to do, Carter projected his guilt at not fulfilling his role into pressure on his son, who could not take it. In 1778 Carter suddenly escaped his role by converting to the Baptists. They

offered him a new culture in which he felt free of the role as
hierarch which had plagued him all his life. Joyfully, he testified before huge public meetings of plain farmers. They, too,
presumably could enjoy the same freedom. Late in life Robert
Carter ran still further away. He spent his last years as a Swe-
denborgian in exile in Baltimore. Having freed all his slaves,
he was safe.

Neither William Byrd nor Landon Carter appears to have
had happy memories of his school days abroad. Neither sent
his sons away to England on the same assignment. Byrd did
not even send his son, William III, away to William and Mary,
where he would have been a contemporary of Robert Carter.
But whether at William and Mary or not, William III only
posed the problem in a new form. Educated at home by tutors, he seems to have learned only two things. One, that a
concern over debt was the last characteristic of a true gentleman. The converse of this was that a blithe extravagance, especially where horses were concerned, was the first feature of
an unimpeachable gentleman. Second, he seems to have concluded like many others that England was the font of cultural
salvation for a gentleman raised in the aspirations of Virginia
society. Accordingly he abandoned his family and spent five
years in pursuit of a commission as an officer in the British
army. But as a colonial he could never get a commission. Neither could his friend and contemporary George Washington
ever succeed in this enterprise. Hopelessly in debt on a scale
his father never imagined, in military disgrace, and unable to
face the agony of being torn both ways by the American
Revolution, William Byrd III committed suicide on New
Year's Day, 1777.

His father's residual insecurities may have come down on
him in his youth, as similar furies were even then descending
on his contemporary Robert Carter's younger sons at almost
as great a cost. This inherited pressure, combined with the
distortions of an education which appears to have led him
to borrow only parts of the all-embracing English model,

namely, extravagance and anglophilia, seems to have undone William Byrd III utterly. Should we see in him the ultimate victim of the processes of provincial education? If so, he may have had company. When in 1766 it was found that extravagant planters had secretly "borrowed" the entire public treasury of £100,000 from Speaker of the House John Robinson, William Byrd III was only the largest of many debtors of a literally bankrupt generation.[242] Were all these debtors the victims of a provincial education as well? Was it such victims who reacted with a rigid fear of chaos when challenged by the Baptists in Virginia in the 1760s and 1770s?[243] Small wonder that by Edmund Ruffin's time, early in the nineteenth century, tidewater culture was to be as sterile as it thought its soil was.[244]

The irony in all of this is the irony of an act of cultural construction which brought destruction to its own constructors. Cultures, taken rigidly, do not act kindly to those who would borrow them for new contexts. But such rigidity is precisely what wholesale cultural borrowing involves, so some destruction is inevitable. Virginia's indigenous culture would therefore be even slower to mature than were William Byrd or Landon Carter as individuals. Some would argue that, like Robert Carter, Virginia's culture never did truly mature. In this view, it was a brilliant, brittle attempt to do the impossible in cultural terms. Even if it had matured, it was doomed by the coming of lubberland. Where did *this* Virginia culture mature if it matured at all? Perhaps in William Byrd II's *History of the Dividing Line,* in which one of its near cripples gave it graceful form.

Yet the destruction was not complete. While Byrd's *History* was never published in his lifetime, and in this sense remained a failed monument to the potential maturity of a too-brittle gentry, from another perspective Byrd's personal evolution, and his *History of the Dividing Line,* were among the first landmarks in what was ultimately to be a costly but successful process of cultural adaptation for the Virginia gentry. Byrd's tragedy never quite became a tragedy nor, despite all its later debts and suicides, and despite the fatalism which by the early nineteenth century infected those Virginia gentlemen left behind in the tidewater, did the potential tragedy of his class ever quite complete itself. Byrd and many of his fellow gentry were simply too resourceful to succumb.

From the beginning, William Byrd himself had eluded the worst pressures of his youth by developing a charming transparency which made even his enemies—exactly as he had suggested in "Inamorato L'Oiseaux"—become his friends. Sir John Perceval was not pleased with Byrd's portrait of their mentor, Southwell, but remained a correspondent. Some members of the Virginia Council were frightened by Byrd's ambition to be governor, but they welcomed back a defeated Byrd with open arms and substantially without reprisals. Byrd and Spotswood lived long enough to become friends, and Spotswood clearly welcomed his friendship. Despite the pressure of his upbringing, Byrd had not only the resourcefulness to be charming, and in the process subtly to reveal himself, but also the inner resources finally to accept defeat and to remake himself in the more limited image of the Virginia gentleman. It is hard to consider this adapted gentleman, eagerly courting burgesses and talking with his slaves, as a failure.

In one vital respect Byrd's adaptation was to be a harbinger of the Virginia gentry's eventual success in adapting its self-image to New World circumstances. Explicitly in his *Secret History* and implicitly in his *History of the Dividing Line* he offered a portrait of himself as "Steddy," a model for a calm, cheerful, persistent, and almost spartan gentleman. This sort of gentleman, he seemed to say, deeply responsive to the needs of those around him and persistent in his duty, was suitable for and indeed desperately needed in the New World. True American woodsmen did not need to be patronized, let alone browbeaten, and they respected a leader who shared their hardships while showing them how to overcome the literal and social wildernesses of the New World. There were contradictions in Byrd's stance, for at the same moment he was writing his histories he was conceiving an impressive edifice at Westover and trying to import obedient German-Swiss settlers for his western estates. Like the Virginia gentry as a whole, Byrd was nothing if not deeply contradictory, even in his maturity. Yet in his histories he appears to have been taking one of the first explicit steps toward adapting the English model of a gentleman's role to the lesser scale and more democratic conditions of American life.

By so redefining the gentry's role, William Byrd made himself part of a wider process of adaptation by which the Virginia gentry became the responsible if not always the spartan leaders of a worthy Virginia populace. This process had already begun from beneath William Byrd, as it were, even before Byrd's own conversion was complete. It had begun in the slowly evolving subculture of the House of Burgesses, members of which toward the end of the seventeenth century already had shown signs of developing a new sense of responsibility toward their constituents, the ordinary yeomen and small planters of Virginia.[245] Alexander Spotswood's later remark to the contrary notwithstanding, increasingly the burgesses were not a "mean" lot at all. By the early eighteenth century, what might be called the county gentry, members of the social layer beneath the great magnates who dominated the society and the Council, were becoming men of substance, experience, and style.[246] These county gentlemen were joined as burgesses by the sons and sons-in-law of the great men on the Council. It was the burgesses who would best embody the portrait of a "steddy" gentry first explicitly sketched by William Byrd.

The House of Burgesses had swept into the forefront of Virginia politics in the years 1714–1720, in the course of the long battle with Alexander Spotswood.[247] The Burgesses' leadership of Virginia politics came about because, until 1717,

the Council was too divided, and its anti-Spotswood majority
too cautious, to declare all-out political war on their governor. When finally the majority did war on Spotswood, their
preoccupation remained with their own prerogatives as councillors, as auditors and receivers, and as judges. In Byrd's case,
the Council's prerogatives were in turn merely a springboard
for his own ambition to become governor. In the meantime
the new House of Burgesses seated in 1715 sought to revoke
the main items in Spotswood's list of legislation, and opposed
his attempts to tamper with elections and with their own
membership. In the process the House snapped up the oppor-
tunistic Byrd and made him their agent, in which capacity he
had been rather more successful than as erstwhile "agent"
for a cautious Council. When, in 1719, Byrd and the Council
were instructed by an exasperated Board of Trade to compromise their particular differences with Spotswood, the Council found itself in effect forbidden by the Board to oppose
Spotswood any longer. At this point, the opposition members
of the Council felt they had no choice but to follow Byrd, hat
in hand, to the Burgesses and to seek their support in continuing the battle with Spotswood over the issues which most concerned the Council. The Burgesses were willing enough to
have the Council's support, but the emphasis within this
new alliance tended to shift to the Burgesses' concerns. From
this moment on, the Council lost the political initiative to
the House of Burgesses. It was, thus, almost an anticlimax
when in 1722 the Anglican church's commissary in Virginia,
James Blair, gave Spotswood the death stroke over largely un-
related issues, which were of concern chiefly to the Anglican
church. By then, the Burgesses' opposition had already neu-
tered the governor.

What is significant is that after its victories over Alexander
Spotswood the House of Burgesses went on under the deferential William Gooch to develop an ever more explicit sense
of its own powers and traditions, which were themselves an
adaptation of parliamentary traditions to Virginia circum-

stances. Most remarkably, the House, conscious of its central role in Virginia politics, also developed a wider conception of the need for a responsive and responsible Virginia gentry in whose hands that power could safely be placed. This conception of gentry responsibility was very much like William Byrd's ideal model of a "steddy" New World gentry, as evolved in his histories. The emerging sense of responsibility was sustained by the well-crafted legislation of the House of Burgesses over the next two generations. The widely enfranchised yeomen of Virginia deferred consistently to the gentlemen they sent to the House of Burgesses because these gentlemen met their constituents' needs as well as their own through acts which established the lines of consensual social order. Mutual trust, and a remarkable harmony, were to characterize Virginia politics almost uniquely in the Anglo-American world in the latter part of the eighteenth century.[248]

There was of course a continuing struggle in Virginia politics, as there had been within William Byrd himself, between the raw arrogance of a nouveau riche planter class stiff with imitative gentility, rather defensively imposing a rigid model of its role on itself and on its inferiors, and the growing effort to temper this vulnerable brittleness with a tradition of political service appropriate to Virginia's wide constituency of enfranchised yeomen. In the end, despite the challenges of constant public scrutiny and increasing debt, the Virginia gentry successfully maintained their new credentials of responsibility, so carefully cultivated in the House of Burgesses. One landmark of their success can be seen in the way the House handled the aftermath of the Robinson scandal of 1766. The late John Robinson, Speaker of the House and a political "manager" of dimensions approaching those of the notorious aristocratic managers of the English Parliament, had shown a most useful pity when he had loaned the entire public treasury to such extravagant and nearly bankrupt planters as William Byrd III. The accumulated pressures of preserving both the image of English gentlemen in Virginia and his own management of the House had led Robinson simply to ignore the traditions of public accountability cultivated by the House. But in the end Robinson's political corruption and his clients' doomed extravagance could not prevail, for in 1766 other burgesses stepped forward, led by Edmund Pendleton of Caroline County, to repair the damage done by Robinson and his clients. It took Pendleton and the Burgesses fifteen years, but by 1781 the entire debt of £100,000 had been repaid to the public treasury of Virginia. It was painful, and it was difficult, and along the way the sense of shame and the pressure to settle his debt may have been what pushed William Byrd III over the brink to suicide, but the House ensured that responsibility triumphed.[249]

So the Virginians' tendency to "political mimesis," as one historian has called it, did not simply result in some cases, as with William Byrd II's early career, in brittleness and in others, as with William Byrd III, in a disastrous extravagance.[250] Mimesis was also, in William Byrd II himself and after him in the House of Burgesses, a process of creative adaptation on the part of men increasingly aware that only a responsible gentry could prevail in an America where most white men were relatively independent and were enfranchised. In fact, the Virginia planters' responsible exercise of political power in the House of Burgesses became in a sense the focus of their only truly indigenous political and social culture.

By the time of the American Revolution to be a Virginia gentleman was above all to be educated in the deeply responsible, indigenous political traditions of the House of Burgesses.[251] By this time, in this new definition of "gentleman" only minimal other qualifications were required. Patrick Henry was too poor to go to England for an education, or even to William and Mary. He could never have become a Virginia gentleman under the broader English model which had for so long dominated Virginia gentry culture. Nor would he have wanted to. For, thanks to political and social changes which took place in the eighteenth century, he could enter the

House of Burgesses as a near gentleman willing to be schooled in the traditions of that House.[252] Educated in this school, he came to dominate Virginia politics. In this adapted politics, and dating from the departure of Sir Alexander Spotswood, the Virginia gentry found its nature, and its true culture. Open, flexible, natural to their environment, it was the first great metaphorical flexing of the rigidly preceptual version of the model of the English gentleman which had rendered so tragically brittle the rest of their culture.

The piedmont planters Thomas Jefferson and James Madison were perhaps more representative products of the House than was Patrick Henry. Of the two, Madison was the more creative, for in his *Federalist #10* he momentarily glimpsed a future in which even the "enlightened statesmen" of his class might no longer be called upon to lead the people.[253] In Madison's view, the mechanisms of the new federal constitution he had done so much to shape would guarantee a stable, just, and democratic society even without a class of responsible gentlemen at the helm. In a sense, Madison, who had been raised in the Virginia political culture centered on the House of Burgesses, saw it as his highest responsibility to provide the new nation with a form of representative government which no longer required men such as himself. In this act, the Virginians' ever more supple metaphor of gentility flexed itself potentially out of existence. Within Virginia, however, for a long time no such extreme adaptations to the tide of revolutionary democracy were needed. If not always the tidewater, then at least the piedmont gentlemen of Madison's generation continued to play a large role in the governance of the new state of Virginia long after the Revolution. This, too, was a testimony to their adaptability.

What the story of William Byrd II does is not so much to elucidate the origins of the well-known political adaptability of the later Virginia gentry, however, as to expose again the price the gentry paid for achieving that adaptability. One price, as is well known, was slavery. Virginia's gentlemen purchased their leadership, and their responsibility for the liberties of white Virginians, with a system of slavery that was to give their descendants severe problems in a future day of reckoning.[254] Less well known is the price they paid from the beginning, in the personal and cultural destructions consequent on their recurring need to borrow a perfect model of English gentry culture in order to maintain their hegemony in Virginia. In William Byrd II the pressures of adopting that model wreaked great personal damage. In Landon Carter they caused continual strain. In Robert Carter such pressures appear nearly to have brought personal destruction. In William Byrd III a distorted—or a rebellious—pursuit of the English gentleman's extravagance alone, a pursuit typical of his generation, finally did bring physical destruction.[255] These names make it impossible to forget at what high costs ruling Virginians finally wrought their changes on the theme of gentility.

Notes

* Elizabeth and Walter Hayes were the original inspiration for this essay in its first form as a screenplay we wrote together. Since then Greg Dening, Rhys Isaac, Colleen Isaac, Donna Merwick, and Suzanne O'Callaghan, together with many others in Melbourne and Adelaide, have provided the support, inspiration, and intellectual framework which have made its completion possible. John Stagg, Jan Lewis, Thad Tate, Stephen Botein, Jacob Price, Andrew Watson, John Shy, John Demos, Bryn Roberts, Ian Steele, Neville Thompson, Robert Gross, and Maris Vinovskis have also read the manuscript and have given me many constructive insights. So has my wife, Helena Hoas, whose reactions on hearing it read each day were the surest guide to telling the story. Our friends, colleagues, and neighbors in Auckland and in Melbourne offered the laughter and calm any story needs for its completion. Di Olle, Cheri Bull, Patty Brennan, and Joan Mathews helped get the manuscript into presentable shape, and the University of Michigan, the University of Auckland, the Australian-American Educational Foundation, the University of Melbourne, and La Trobe University provided the financial support which made it all possible. John D'Arms, Dean of the Rackham School of Graduate Studies at the University of Michigan, provided a quiet place in which to do revisions. The present story is an offering of gratitude to them all.

1. *The Secret Diary of William Byrd of Westover, 1709–1712*, ed. Louis B. Wright and Marion Tinling (Richmond, Va., 1941), hereafter cited as *Secret Diary*; *William Byrd of Virginia: The London Diary (1717–1721) and Other Writings*, ed. Louis B. Wright and Marion Tinling (New York, 1958), hereafter *London Diary*; and *Another Secret Diary of William Byrd of Westover, 1739–1741: With Letters and Literary Exercises, 1696–1726*, ed. Maude H. Woodfin, trans. Marion Tinling (Richmond, Va., 1942), hereafter *Another Secret Diary*. The purveyance and appearance of the diaries are discussed in the editorial introductions by Wright, Tinling, and Woodfin, with whose editorial judgments, as far as they go, this author largely agrees. Wright's introduction to the *London Diary* is the best short life of William Byrd. His views on all editorial questions are largely confirmed and his life of Byrd much extended in Pierre Marambaud's excellent treatment of Byrd as a literary and cul-

tural figure, *William Byrd of Westover, 1674–1744* (Charlottesville, Va., 1971). Marambaud discusses the rare occasions on which Byrd failed to make an entry in his diary (p. 115).

2. Again, Louis B. Wright, Marion Tinling, Maude Woodfin, and Pierre Marambaud (see note 1, above), substantiate the facts and interpretation offered here. That Byrd never mentioned the diary or made provision for its preservation is based on the three published diaries, on the literary exercises printed with *Another Secret Diary*, on *The Correspondence of the Three William Byrds of Westover, Virginia, 1684–1776*, ed. Marion Tinling, 2 vols. (Charlottesville, Va., 1977), hereafter cited as *Correspondence*, and on the other sources cited below.

3. For a physical description of the diaries, see figure 1 and the works cited in note 1, above.

4. See the editorial introductions to the published diaries cited above. The regularity of the routine seen in the early diary and the significance of breaches in that routine are beautifully set forth in an unpublished paper by Zhu Zhao Chen, "Care or Carelessness: William Byrd and His Wife and His Children: An Approach to Understanding William Byrd through His Diary," written for Rhys Isaac at La Trobe University, 1984.

5. See the text below for a treatment of the changes in this routine and in the diary as a whole over time.

6. In *Richard Steele* (Boston, 1982), Richard H. Dammers discusses the philosophy behind the *Tatler* and the *Spectator*, a philosophy best summed up in *Spectator* no. 75. That Byrd read the *Tatler* is seen in the *Secret Diary*, July 8, 1710; the loss of tobacco at sea was on May 6, 1709; his quarrels with his wife are characterized below; the death of his son was on June 3, 1710.

7. See, for example, *Secret Diary*, May 12 and 13, 20 and 21, 28 and 29, 1710.

8. For the loss of the tobacco shipment, see *ibid.*, May 6, 1709; for the quarrel with Lucy, see *ibid.*, April 8, 1709.

9. See note 6 and examples from the diary cited above.

10. *The Diary of Samuel Pepys*, ed. Robert Latham and William Matthews (London, 1970–1983); for further comments on Pepys and for Evelyn and Ryder, see Robert A. Fothergill, *Private Chronicles: A Study of English Diaries* (London, 1974); for Rose, see *The Diary of Robert Rose: A View of Virginia by a Scottish Colonial Parson, 1746–1751*, ed. Ralph Emmett Fall (Verona, Va., 1977).

11. See Fothergill, *Private Chronicles*, and Elisabeth Bourcier, *Les*

journaux privés en Angleterre de 1600 à 1660 (Lille, 1977; Ph.D. thesis, Université de Paris IV, 1971).

12. For the Virginia view, see the final paragraph of Louis B. Wright's introduction to the *London Diary;* Matthews's observation is in the *Diary of Samuel Pepys,* I, cx; the Fothergill quotation is from *Private Chronicles,* 28.

13. Lawrence Stone, *The Family, Sex, and Marriage in England, 1500– 1800* (London, 1977), 563; Michael Zuckerman, "William Byrd's Family," *Perspectives in American History,* XII (1979), 253–311; and above all, Zuckerman, "Fate, Flux, and Good Fellowship: An Early Virginia Design for the Dilemma of American Business," in *Business and Its Environment: Essays for Thomas C. Cochran,* ed. Harold Issadore Sharlin (Westport, Conn., 1983), 161–184. For the analysis of variations, see the paper by Chen cited in note 4, above. As will be seen, Zuckerman was perhaps mistaken in both the conclusions mentioned here, but there is an ultimate sense in which he was right in portraying Byrd as somehow brittle and in recognizing that this quality must be related to Byrd's position as a New World gentleman. Other historians have mined Byrd's diaries for quotations, but none of them has sought to decode the man and his life and writings directly. In this perspective, Zuckerman and Chen are the best analyses to date. Marambaud's *William Byrd* is very useful, but so fragments the man as nearly to evade his personality and the organic nature of his life.

14. These other writings are in the *Correspondence* volumes and in *Another Secret Diary;* all will be discussed in more detail below.

15. See, for example, the works by Wright, Marambaud, Stone, and Zuckerman cited above. The portrait will be substantiated and developed at length in the text below.

16. Documented in Louis B. Wright, *The First Gentlemen of Virginia: Intellectual Qualities of the Early Colonial Ruling Class* (San Marino, Calif., 1940), 320, and in Wright's introduction to the *London Diary,* 8. The evidence for the following hypothetical reconstruction of a childhood consistent with William Byrd's personality as a young man is largely circumstantial, but is spelled out in the subsequent pages and gains much confirmation from later episodes in this narrative. The theoretical basis for this relating of his childhood circumstances to Byrd's early adult personality will be found in note 25, below, and is amplified later, at the appropriate points in the narrative, in notes 173 and 177. As the subsequent text and these latter notes will show, however, there is no

rigid determinism to the view of personality offered here, for insofar as Byrd's childhood and youth embodied in part a pathology, he nonetheless substantially outgrew that handicap through a difficult and complex process of maturation. It is also possible that events before or just after Byrd's school years were equally influential in shaping the early personality which emerges by 1695 or so, but there is scarcely ever circumstantial evidence for those periods of his life. Byrd's life in general until he is sixteen or even twenty is very sparsely documented.

17. See the text for the years 1705–1710, below.

18. What follows is based on Louis B. Wright's portrait "William Byrd I" and on the letters included thereafter in *Correspondence*, I, 3–191.

19. Bacon's speech is in Warren M. Billings, ed., *The Old Dominion in the Seventeenth Century: A Documentary History of Virginia, 1606–1689* (Chapel Hill, N.C., 1975), 278. William Byrd I did reveal his motives a bit when he said, subsequently, having sent his youngest daughter to England for an education, "shee could learne nothing good here, in a great family of Negro's" (*Correspondence*, I, 32).

20. Byrd's sister Ursula was consigned to relatives with the words quoted in this paragraph on March 31, 1685 (*Correspondence*, I, 33). For Felsted, see Michael Craze, *A History of Felsted School, 1564–1947* (Ipswich, 1955), 1–100. Daniel Horsmanden's complaint and Byrd I's response suggest a running dispute over the direct care of Byrd's daughters Ursula and Susan, which, with the role of advisor to William Byrd II, had by 1690 fallen upon Horsmanden (*Correspondence*, I, 152). William Byrd II's later letters do not indicate that either Warham or Daniel Horsmanden were close mentors or fondly remembered. Of the scores of surviving letters none is from or to either man, nor is either man ever mentioned in this capacity in Byrd's letters, even though the full range of Byrd's family and acquaintances is otherwise well represented. Further, Byrd's diaries do not treat either of the older Horsmandens in this light.

21. The elder Byrds' greetings are found throughout *Correspondence*, I, 8–164; for the two letters from Byrd senior to Byrd junior, see *ibid.*, 35, 123.

22. For an example, see Craze, *History of Felsted School*, 42–43.

23. *Correspondence*, I, 12–125, documents Byrd I's pursuit of office by letter and through his visit to London in 1687, of which, unfortunately, virtually nothing else is known; see especially pp. 25, 71, 81, 93, 102, 105. Byrd junior also saw his father on a brief visit to Virginia in 1696–1697.

24. That such was the purpose of Felsted School can be seen in Craze, *History of Felsted School*, 1–100.

25. For the grandfather and uncle, see note 20, above. Glasscock was nearly 70 when Byrd arrived and was in ill health before his death at 79 in 1690; see Craze, *History of Felsted School*. Again, "no man emerged" as mentor by the same definition applied in note 20, above; neither in Byrd's letters in the *Correspondence* nor in his writings or diary does he speak of such a figure. Aside from three routine references to Daniel Horsmanden senior in October 1718 in the *London Diary*, Byrd never referred in later life to any man whom he knew during his school days.

The entire theory implicit in this and the following paragraphs, as of this entire essay, is based on the insights of George Herbert Mead, as published in *On Social Psychology: Selected Papers*, ed. Anselm Strauss (Chicago, 1964). Mead's whole definition of personal maturity centers on the ability of the individual, through relationships with "significant others," to define the social patterns of individual conduct in a broad and general sense, affording scope for flexibility. By implication, in Mead's view, failure to learn through such relationships can lead the individual to uphold narrow definitions of fixed and specific patterns of acting. Mead's social and cultural definition of maturity has been vastly extended by Peter L. Berger and Thomas Luckmann in *The Social Construction of Reality: A Treatise in the Sociology of Knowledge* (Garden City, N.Y., 1966). Berger and Luckmann (pp. 161–171) also imply a pathology of personalities which for various reasons fail to mature by means of early relationships with significant others through which they can learn to internalize the social roles they must play in a flexible and "distanced" (in this text hereafter referred to as "metaphorical" and discussed further in the text and in note 177, below) manner. Professor Greg Dening of Melbourne University first suggested the application of this pathology to William Byrd II's early life, and in so doing extended Berger and Luckmann's typology of pathologies explicitly to include cases such as Byrd's, where "significant others" are simply lacking and therefore both learning and identity are rigidly "preceptual."

Since the latter term will eventually be applied to the personality which emerged from Byrd's school days, it might be well to define it now. By "preceptual" is meant the tendency to learn a role as a series of precepts, specific behaviors learned usually from books, by rote, or as abstract examples, the rigid and continual practice of which is thought to

constitute the successful fulfillment of the role in question. Because of
his circumstances at Felsted, in this hypothesis, William Byrd began
with a preceptual concept of his desired role, that of an English gentleman. Through a long process of maturation, he finally learned a more
appropriate role, that of Virginia gentleman, "metaphorically"—that is,
learned from his peers in Virginia. He learned that gentility was a metaphor for a subtle and varied state of being, which could be achieved by
flexible and even creative behaviors far transcending the obsessive prac-
ticing of rigid precepts. The rest of this process in Byrd's life is detailed in
the text, and the theory is extended in notes 173 and 177, below. It is this
version of the Mead/Berger-Luckmann theory which is used throughout
this essay.

26. In the sources cited in note 20, above.

27. The Southwell and Perceval acquaintanceships are documented in
Another Secret Diary, xvi, xix–xx, 191–192, 206–208, and in the later
letters between Perceval and Byrd II in the *Correspondence* volumes.

28. *Secret Diary*, June 22, 1710; see further discussion below.

29. For the Middle Temple inscription, see *Correspondence*, I, 167; for
Lynde, see *ibid.*, II, 473–474.

30. In further explication of Byrd's school environment, it should be
observed that *none* of the boys on the 1710 student list, the first available, seems to have been from the colonies. Byrd was, then, unusual in
coming not only from outside Essex but from outside England; see
Craze, *History of Felsted School*, 15–115, for this information. That Englishmen were ignorant of the colonies can be seen in Robert Beverley's
introduction to his *History and Present State of Virginia* (London, 1705)
and in the "Autobiography of the Reverend John Barnard (1767)," ex-
cerpted in John Demos, ed., *Remarkable Providences, 1600–1760* (New
York, 1972). On Byrd's sensitivity to slights, see "Inamorato L'Oiseaux"
in *Another Secret Diary*, 276–282; see also the treatment of his 1718
romance with "Sabina," below.

31. *Correspondence*, II, 580, 603.

32. For the Old School Room, again, see Craze, *History of Felsted
School*, 48; for this view of Byrd in general, see Wright's introduction to
the *London Diary* and Marambaud's *William Byrd*; the solitude is documented in the text's ensuing discussion of Byrd's days in the context of
the diary for 1709–1712; and the contents of Byrd's library are listed in
The Writings of "Colonel William Byrd, of Westover in Virginia, Esqr.,"

ed. John Spencer Bassett (New York, 1901), appendix A. The catalog Bassett gives is a later sale catalog and leaves much to be desired.

33. The conditions of Byrd's school days are documented in the text and notes above; the theory of the personal pathology on which this interpretation is based is explained in note 25, above; and the resultant personality and behavior are discussed and documented in full in the text below.

34. Thomas Elyot, *The Boke Named the Governour* (London, 1580 [orig. publ. 1531]); Richard Brathwait, *The English Gentleman* (London, 1630; facsimile reprint, Norwood, N.J., 1975). Lotte Mulligan and Judith Richards of La Trobe University very kindly suggested these as possible sources of Byrd's routine.

35. Elyot, *Boke Named the Governour*, 156–157; for Byrd's reading, see for example the index to the *Secret Diary* under "Lucian" and "Homer." The later diaries are less well indexed but the frequencies of these readings equally high.

36. Elyot, *Boke Named the Governour*, 238–269; for T'ai-chi, see Anna Seidel, "A Taoist Immortal of the Ming Dynasty: Chang San-feng," in Wm. Theodore de Bary *et al.*, *Self and Society in Ming Thought* (New York, 1970), 504–506. T'ai-chi had its origins in self-defense disciplines, but the end result in the form of present T'ai-chi is very like what Elyot describes. Elyot's version is evidently unknown as a Western cultural tradition.

37. Brathwait, *English Gentleman*, 233ff.; *Secret Diary*, throughout. For examples of "most English gentlemen" in practice, see Thomas Ellwood, *The History of the Life of Thomas Ellwood: Written by Himself* (London, 1827 [orig. publ. 1714]), and *The Oxinden and Peyton Letters, 1642–1670: Being the Correspondence of Henry Oxinden of Barham, Sir Thomas Peyton of Knowlton and Their Circle*, ed. Dorothy Gardiner (London, 1937). That an almost compulsive social round was more generally characteristic of English gentlemen is seen in Lawrence Stone and Jeanne C. Fawtier Stone, *An Open Elite? England, 1540–1880* (Oxford, 1984), 307–308.

38. Brathwait, *English Gentleman*, 401.

39. *Ibid.*, 457–459; *Another Secret Diary*, 206–207 and notes.

40. For Byrd I, see *Correspondence*, I, 178. Byrd's pursuit of a governorship and his dreams are best documented by referring to the entry for William Byrd II in the index to the *Secret Diary*. Specific examples of

both are cited in the text and in note 64, below. Note that the "governorship" sought was sometimes technically the lieutenant governorship, in cases where the formal governorship was held as a sinecure by an influential lord in England. But the effective power and distinction were the same, as was the de facto title in Virginia. Lucy's father is discussed both in Wright's introduction to the *London Diary* and in Marambaud, *William Byrd*. Byrd's early friends John Campbell, later duke of Argyll, John Perceval, later earl of Egmont, and Charles Wager, later Sir Charles, all eventually rose to the top ranks of command in England; for discussion of these men, see index to the *Correspondence* volumes and Wright's introduction to the *London Diary*.

41. For examples of rejections, see the discussion of the duke of Marlborough's reply in 1710 and of "Sabina's" father's reaction in 1718, in the text below; the details are in the *Secret Diary*, March 31, 1710, and *Another Secret Diary*, 318. (Note that *page* references to *Another Secret Diary* do not refer to the diary of 1739–1741 but to the earlier writings included in the same volume.) What follows in this paragraph of text is, again, a sketch of behaviors which will be demonstrated in detail in the course of this essay. The theoretical background for this analysis of Byrd's personality, and of the terms "precept" and "metaphor," can be found in note 25, above, and in the text and note 177, below.

42. *Another Secret Diary*, 276–282 and notes. All quotations in the text to the end of this section are from "Inamorato L'Oiseaux."

43. The commonplace book is in the Virginia Historical Society; the judgment on it delivered here is that of Louis B. Wright in his introduction to *The Prose Works of William Byrd of Westover: Narrative of a Colonial Virginian* (Cambridge, Mass., 1966), 37–38, hereafter cited as *Prose Works*. If, and it is a big "if," Byrd's sexual references in his diaries do represent his entire sexual life, then he was possibly sexually self-repressed (save in moments of bragging or of crisis) even while living in London. This is not surprising in view of his constant self-editing. For comments on the possible infrequency of his orgasms, see Stone, *Family, Sex, and Marriage in England*, 563–568.

44. Wright's introduction to *London Diary*; Marambaud, *William Byrd*; and text below.

45. See note 44, above, and *Correspondence*, I, 209ff.; for the journal, see *ibid.*, 213. Bacon's "Of Travel" will be discussed in detail in the text for 1705–1709, below.

46. See *Correspondence*, I, 209ff.; for "Cavaliero Sapiente," see *Another Secret Diary*, 206–208.

47. *Correspondence*, I, 210 n. 1.

48. *Ibid.*, 168.

49. This and the following quotations are taken in sequence, *ibid.*, 216–244.

50. Again, for all quotations see *ibid.*; for the marriage, see *ibid.*, 218 n. 1.

51. All three pieces are in *Another Secret Diary*, on pp. 192–193, 213–214, and 209–211, respectively.

52. *Ibid.*, 356–386, 405–409, and text below.

53. Again, for standard biographical details, see Wright's introduction to the *London Diary*, Marambaud, *William Byrd* (the house is on p. 52), and the text below.

54. For Byrd's journal, see *Correspondence*, I, 213; the Bacon essay is quoted in Fothergill, *Private Chronicles*, 15.

55. William Mason, *A Pen Pluck'd from an Eagles Wing . . .* (London, 1672); *Correspondence*, I, 203–215.

56. Again, Wright, Marambaud, and Woodfin agree that such genres were largely confined to the periods 1690–1705 and 1717–1722 in Byrd's life.

57. See note 56, above, for Byrd's editors' opinions. In a letter to the author of June 19, 1985, Pierre Marambaud confirms that both Byrd's shorthand and his secret diary date from after the publication of Mason's *La plume volante* in 1707. There is, however, a potential reference to cipher in an undated letter which probably *but not certainly* postdates 1707; see *Another Secret Diary*, 263–265. The later references to cipher are in the "Sabina" and "Minionet" exchanges in *Another Secret Diary*, 298ff. and 371ff., and are discussed in the text below.

58. William Byrd I's will is printed in the *Virginia Magazine of History and Biography*, XLVIII (1940), 331–339.

59. What follows is taken in sequence from the *Secret Diary* for December 1, 1709, to March 1, 1710.

60. The *Secret Diary* index under "Byrd, William II" and under "Dreams and portents" is the best way to retrace the evolution of Byrd's dreams. Dreams of death are recorded on April 8, 1709, possibly again on April 14, and again on July 15, 1709.

61. The entire creed is in the *Secret Diary*, xxviii n. 12.

62. This and later references to Virginia's history are based on Richard L. Morton, *Colonial Virginia*, 2 vols. (Chapel Hill, N.C., 1960), unless otherwise specified.

63. Beverley, *History and Present State of Virginia*; for Byrd circa 1726–1727, see *Correspondence*, I, 354–361 (for the rooms and books, see pp. 399–400, 432). For a similar linkage, see also *ibid.*, 384 (1728). For a contemptuous reference to Virginia culture around 1705, see *ibid.*, 257.

64. The satire of the House of Burgesses is chronicled in the *Secret Diary*, November 24, 26, 1710. Again, the pursuit of a governorship or, in some cases, what was technically the lieutenant governorship, is best traced through the index of the *Secret Diary* under "Byrd, William II" and "Dreams and portents" as well as in the *Correspondence* volumes. See, for example, *Secret Diary*, September 16, 19, 1709, March 31, April 17, and August 29, 1710. In a letter to William Blathwayt, Byrd seems to fish for a governorship (*Correspondence*, I, 269), an aim which may also explain a flurry of "scientific" letters to the extremely well connected Dr. Hans Sloane between 1706 and 1709. See also *ibid.*, 324 n. 5, for evidence of continuing efforts. The seriousness and intensity of these efforts stand in marked contrast to the two wistful hintings at a governorship seen after 1726; see, for example, *ibid.*, 358–359, II, 485.

65. See note 54.

66. See *Prose Works*, 37–38.

67. *Secret Diary*, January 22–23, 1710. Anne Harper has since pointed out to me that Byrd may have acquired the idea of using shorthand for secrecy from that most secretive diplomat and plotter of all, John Locke. In *Some Thoughts concerning Education*, published in 1693, shortly after his days as a conspirator had ended in success, Locke recommended shorthand, "both for Dispatch in what Men write for their own Memory, and Concealment of what they would not have lie open to every Eye. For he that has once learn'd any Sort of Character may easily vary it to his own private use of phansy, and with more Contraction suited to the Business he would imploy it in" (paragraph 161, p. 266, James L. Axtell edition, Cambridge, 1968). This work was in Byrd's library.

68. See the discussion of the "Sabina" and "Minionet" romances in the text below.

69. On rejection by women all through Byrd's life, see the romance with Lady Betty Cromwell, chronicled above, and those with "Minionet" and "Sabina," below; for Lucy's listening at the top of the stairs, see *Secret*

Diary, April 8, 1709; for Byrd's refusing to give her a book, see December 30, 1711; on control of his emotions, see the discussion of Byrd's relationship with Lucy in the text following, which also treats the successes of their marriage.

70. See discussion following. The powerful role privacy could play in a marriage of this period, and the close relationship of wealth to personal space and personal space to privacy, are nicely chronicled in Orest Ranum, "Inventing Private Space: Samuel and Mrs. Pepys at Home, 1660–1669," in *Vissenschaftskolleg—Institute for Advanced Study—Zu Berlin, Jahrbuch 1982/3* (Berlin, 1984).

71. See, for example, *Secret Diary,* July 7, 8, and 9, 1709, quoted in the text above.

72. Again, Chen's paper, cited in note 4, above, gives a systematic view of the regularities involved.

73. Byrd's statement that he "loved retirement" is in "Inamorato L'Oiseaux" in *Another Secret Diary,* 218; the rest can be seen in the *Secret Diary.*

74. The *Tatler* and the *Spectator,* for example, *Spectator* no. 75, establish the norm; Byrd's practice of it is exemplified below.

75. Byrd's "composure" with Lucy will be examined in detail below. Unless otherwise noted, all specifically dated quotations in the text are assumed to be from the diary for the relevant period, i.e., the *Secret Diary* for 1709–1712, the *London Diary* for 1717–1721, and *Another Secret Diary* for 1739–1741. Such quotations will not be footnoted.

76. *Secret Diary,* June 23, 1710.

77. *Ibid.,* June 3–11, 1710.

78. *Correspondence,* I, 296.

79. See *Secret Diary* index entry for Lucy Parke Byrd; references to merriment, walks, and visitors occur throughout the diary; the billiard table incident is July 30, 1710; the afternoon of play is November 15, 1709.

80. Again, these relationships should be followed in the index to the *Secret Diary,* under "Oastler" and "Anderson."

81. *Ibid.,* April 10, 1710.

82. *Ibid.,* April 14, 1710.

83. For the two marriages, see *Correspondence,* I, 259 n. 1; the friendship can be followed chiefly through the two men's letters in the *Correspondence* volumes. See also Jo Zuppan, "John Custis of Williamsburg, 1678–1749,"*VMHB,* XC (1982), 177–197.

84. Here, as previously, the references to William Cocke in the index to the *Secret Diary* must be read sequentially to substantiate this relationship; for the tense period, see particularly August 6, 1710 (payment), March 28, 1711 (teasing), and July 1, 1711 (payment); the final reference is from April 25, 1711.

85. *Ibid.*, May 5, July 3, 6, August 31, 1711, January 29, 1712.

86. *Ibid.*, May 13, June 12, March 27, 1711, respectively.

87. *Ibid.*, July 5–18, 1711; for the friend's brother episode, see July 30, 1711.

88. Again, see *Secret Diary* index under "Cocke"; "pleasant company" is December 23, 1711; "merry as we always are," February 17, 1712; for Cocke as family confidante, see April 21, 1712; for Cocke's coach, see April 14, 1712; for the governor's double dealing, see June 10, 1712. See also *Executive Journals of the Council of Colonial Virginia*, ed. H. R. McIlwaine *et al.* (Richmond, Va., 1925–1966), III, 313–317.

89. *Secret Diary*, December 31, 1710.

90. Again, see the quotations in the text to note 63, for examples of a later association of literal death with the figurative death of provincial life in Byrd's mind.

91. The relationship is best traced through the index to the *Secret Diary* under the entry for Lucy Parke Byrd, although it is by no means complete. For the argument about her extravagance, see June 14, 15, 1709, and July 9, 1710; for the argument about her eyebrows, see February 5, 1711.

92. *Ibid.*, January 31, 1711.

93. *Recollections and Private Memoirs of Washington, by His Adopted Son, George Washington Parke Custis, with a Memoir of the Author by His Daughter*, ed. Benson J. Lossing (New York, 1860), 17.

94. *Secret Diary*, July 25, 26, 1710.

95. *Ibid.*, March 2, 1712.

96. *Ibid.*, April 27, 1712; January 19, May 14, 18, 1710, and May 18, 1712, are some examples of these conjugal walks.

97. Numbers of slaves are uncertain and varied, but the diary customarily mentions five or six house slaves at a time. "Several dozen" others at Westover alone is a deduction from the partial inventory of Byrd's estate in *Correspondence*, II, 599. For instances of the usage "had whipped" or "whipped," see *Secret Diary*, March 3, October 8, 1710, May 22, 1712; for usage of "were whipped," see February 8, April 17, May 23, June 10, 1709, August 31, 1710, February 27, 1711.

98. *Ibid.*, December 3, 1709.

99. The context of some of these cases can be worked out by studying the entries "Servants, health of," "Ipecac," "Distemper, epidemic of," and "Medicines" in the index to the *Secret Diary*. That care was the master's role can be seen in the entry for May 26, 1709; that slaves were an extension of the master and his fate, in the entries for December 1710, particularly December 29 and 31.

100. *Ibid.*, February 6, 7, 9, 1709.

101. Rhys Isaac, "Description: A Diary and the Performance in It" (paper delivered to the History and Anthropology Seminar, Melbourne University, April 2, 1985).

102. *Secret Diary*, February 24, 25, 1709.

103. *Ibid.*, July 9, December 18, 1710.

104. *Ibid.*, April 27, 1710.

105. *Ibid.*, October 2, 3, 4, 1711.

106. *Ibid.*, August 28, 1711.

107. Again, the details of Byrd's political career are chronicled in Wright's introduction to the *London Diary* and can be seen under "Byrd, William II" in the index to the *Secret Diary*. The attempts to win the governorship are noted in the text and note 64, above.

108. *Secret Diary*, March 31, 1710.

109. *Ibid.*, June 22–October 24, 1710.

110. The general situation is described in Wright's introduction to the *London Diary*, 17, and in Marambaud, *William Byrd*, 26–28, with further details in the editorial notes to the *Secret Diary* (see index under "Parke, Colonel Daniel II"). "Fobbed off" is in Marambaud, *William Byrd*, 28, and "gave me nothing" in *Secret Diary*, May 25, 1711.

111. For Marlborough's rejection, see *Secret Diary*, March 31, 1710; for the dream about Marlborough, see *ibid.*, August 29, 1710. (Note that Sir William Phips, who became governor of Massachusetts under extraordinary circumstances in 1691, and Daniel Parke, whose governorship of the Leeward Islands came under most extraordinary circumstances, were, in Byrd's time, the exceptions which only proved the general rule that colonials did not become governors. Marlborough spoke the harsh truth.) For Byrd's dreams in general, see *Secret Diary* index under "Dreams and portents"; for the coffin and mourning coach dreams, see *ibid.*, January 16, 19, 1712; for the association between literal death and death of ambitions, see Byrd's creed (*ibid.*, xxviii), and the quotation from 1730 cited in note 63, which is in *Correspondence*, I, 432.

112. For Lucy's displeasure, see *Secret Diary*, February 4, 1712.

113. For "his" inheritance, see *ibid.*, May 25, 1711.

114. The standard work on Spotswood is Leonidas Dodson, *Alexander Spotswood, Governor of Colonial Virginia, 1710–1722* (Philadelphia, 1932); see also *The Official Letters of Alexander Spotswood . . . ,* 2 vols. (Richmond, Va., 1882). For a short account, see Morton, *Colonial Virginia*, II, 409–485; see especially p. 442 ("the King's will") and p. 439 ("mean" Burgesses).

115. "No Governor ought to be trusted," see *Secret Diary*, December 1711–January 1712, particularly January 15, 1712; that Byrd's indiscretion quickly became known, see January 21, 1712.

116. By the spring of 1711 (see *ibid.*, March 31, April 1), Byrd had begun to let doubt if not malice color his previously correct relationship with Mrs. Russell, and by May 5 he was repeating "malicious" gossip that she was pregnant, which by May 11 he plainly considered an object of wit. He seemed still to be reveling in the scandal on October 19, 1711, and possibly on October 28. By December 9, 1711, she seems to have been slandering him.

117. *Official Letters of Spotswood*, II, 8–92, 176–182; Spotswood had been concerned about but had not insisted upon reform of the receiver's place until his falling out with Byrd in 1712.

118. *Correspondence*, I, 287–288.

119. *Ibid.*, 324 n. 5.

120. Harrison to Ludwell, May 15, 1719, is cited *ibid.* The ongoing history of Byrd's trip to England is documented in Wright's introduction to the *London Diary* and is best seen in *Correspondence*, I, 287–353.

121. *Correspondence*, 289 n. 2.

122. Such is the deduction from Marambaud, *William Byrd*, 28, and from the entries for Daniel Parke in the indexes to the *London Diary* and the *Correspondence* volumes; "two years' income" is based on his calculations of income in *Another Secret Diary*, 322–323.

123. Marambaud, *William Byrd*, 28, and *Correspondence*, I, 347. The Lane of Perry and Lane died at about this time, so although some correspondents continued to refer to "Perry and Lane," as indeed the text does here, strictly speaking at some point in 1712 the firm became simply "The Perrys."

124. See *Correspondence*, II, 548, placed in context by Marambaud, *William Byrd*, 54–55; for William Byrd I's dislike of debt, see *Correspondence*, I, 8–191.

125. This and the ensuing discussion of Virginia politics are based on volume II of Morton, *Colonial Virginia*; Dodson, *Alexander Spotswood*; *Official Letters of Spotswood*; and Jack P. Greene, "The Opposition to Lieutenant Governor Alexander Spotswood: 1718," *VMHB*, LXX (1962), 35–42. The "implacable" label cited in the following narrative is in Marambaud, *William Byrd*, 41.

126. *Correspondence*, I, 290–324, traces Byrd's actions in general, as does the *London Diary* for 1717–1719; for the sale of the receivership, see *Correspondence*, I, 292–293.

127. Again, see *Correspondence*, I, 324 n. 5, and Byrd's forced disclaimer, *ibid.*, 325. Scarcely anything else could explain Byrd's continuing presence before the Board of Trade at the risk of every office he held. Few 18th-century gentlemen had *so* disinterested a desire for justice as to pursue such a campaign at great loss and risk without some thought of personal gain, and both Nathaniel Harrison and Byrd (as noted, *ibid.*, 324–325) testified to the prevalence of rumors that the governorship was Byrd's goal.

128. See note 126, above, and Wright's introduction to the *London Diary*, 31–32, for the general course of Byrd's campaign; the most detailed account is Marambaud, *William Byrd*, 37–43, which documents Spotswood's effort to remove "that implacable gentleman Byrd" from the Council (p. 41).

129. *Correspondence*, I, 296; Lucy's arrival is noted on p. 293.

130. All dated quotations from 1717–1721 in the text are from the *London Diary* and will not be specifically footnoted.

131. Marambaud, *William Byrd*, 41, gives the best overview of this process.

132. Lawrence Stone does perceive from the "cold" entries of this "unrevealing" diary, whose sporadic, restless sexual excursions he enumerates, that Byrd was a desperately lonely man (*Family, Sex, and Marriage in England*, 563–568). Byrd's history, as chronicled in this essay, explains why. In the perspective of that history, the diary is not "unrevealing" at all, nor is it entirely "cold." As Stone begins to understand, it is the testament of a great personal agony. Like all laconic diaries, it suffers by comparison with the verbosities of Pepys or Boswell, but it has a muted eloquence.

133. See particularly, *Correspondence*, I, 306, where Byrd speaks of a success "not . . . unacceptable to the country in general"; in two letters to Philip Ludwell in 1717 and 1718 one can see Byrd twisting and turn-

ing between the Council, Spotswood, and his own ambitions (*ibid.,* 308–311); then, in a letter to Custis on May 16, 1719, in the midst of imminent failure, he speaks of "a victory I hope will prove an earnest of a much greater" (*ibid.,* 323). As it was in politics, in these letters, so, one feels, it was in the restless round of the diary in 1717–1719, which seems to be at heart a waiting, and a search for a stunning success with the Parke estate, in politics, or in marriage.

134. Sabina to Veramour, July 1, 1717 (*Another Secret Diary,* 301–302). This romance is documented *ibid.,* 298–359 (see especially 298 n. 2).

135. *Ibid.,* 306.

136. Sabina to Veramour, July 10, 1717 (*ibid.,* 306–307).

137. *Ibid.,* 307, 308.

138. *Ibid.,* 313–315.

139. Sabina to Veramour, January 23, 1718 (*ibid.,* 315–316).

140. For Byrd's preparation, see *London Diary,* February 1718, and *Correspondence,* I, 313–314. For the application itself, see *Another Secret Diary,* 321–324, and *Correspondence,* I, 311–313. For Byrd's attempt to borrow money, see *Another Secret Diary,* 341 n. 1. Perceval's and Ned Southwell's behavior toward Byrd is chronicled in the text above, in the context of Byrd's early portrait of Sir Robert Southwell.

141. *Another Secret Diary,* 326. So much did Byrd hold to these "Rules" that he did not even *dream* of actual intercourse with Sabina until the romance was over, when he was "rogering" her in a dream as his revenge; for the details, see Stone, *Family, Sex, and Marriage in England,* 564–565.

142. *Another Secret Diary,* 318.

143. *Ibid.,* 329, 330.

144. *Ibid.,* 336. For further evidence of his disintegration, also from the diary, see *ibid.,* 342 n. 1, 346 n. 1. One suspects from this evidence that agonized hours of composition lay behind *all* of Byrd's serious love letters.

145. See *ibid.,* 339–341, especially 339 n. 1; the quotation is from the *London Diary,* March 31, 1718.

146. *Another Secret Diary,* 347–348; *London Diary,* April 16, 1718.

147. *Another Secret Diary,* 349, 351–354, 357.

148. *Ibid.,* 356 (the references on this page are to the *London Diary,* May 7–19, 1718).

149. For the genre in general from 1717 on, see *Another Secret Diary* for the dating of Byrd's manuscripts; "Dulchetti" is in *Another Secret Diary*, 203–204; some of the poems from "Tunbrigalia" are *ibid.*, 397–409.

150. *Ibid.*, 202–203. The unexplained peak of sexual activity in September 1718 noted in Stone, *Family, Sex, and Marriage in England*, 563–568, may have been another expression of the way Sabina turned Byrd's need to anger.

151. Again, the best account is Marambaud, *William Byrd*, 40–42, but see also *Correspondence*, I, 314–326, and *Another Secret Diary*, 203 n. 2.

152. For the letter to the Board of Trade, see *Correspondence*, I, 320–322; for the letter to Argyll, see *ibid.*, 324–326.

153. The dreams are in the *London Diary*, December 21, 26, 29, 1719, January 7, 26, 1720.

154. A general account of the debt is in Marambaud, *William Byrd*, 28. What is not clear from this account is that it was Micajah the younger who ran the firm after 1721, became "the Alderman," and pursued Byrd nearly until his death. See *London Diary*, 50 n. 7; Jacob M. Price, "The Excise Affair Revisited: The Administrative and Colonial Dimensions of a Parliamentary Crisis," in *England's Rise to Greatness, 1660–1763*, ed. Stephen B. Baxter (Berkeley, Calif., 1983), 257–321; and *Correspondence*, II, 484–485.

155. *Correspondence*, I, 326.

156. For the chariot, see *London Diary*, November 7, 1719; for Byrd's preparations in general, packing, and arranging Argyll's letter, etc., see *ibid.*, November 4–30, 1719; for Annie Wilkinson, see the index, *ibid.*; she may be "the maid" referred to on November 27, 28, 29, and on December 2 and 8, and is possibly the Annie present on December 18 and thereafter a target of Byrd's advances; the other maid was Hannah (*ibid.*, December 10, 26, 1719); "a terrible noise in the night," again, is November 14, 1719; for the long goodbyes, see especially November 27–28, 1719.

157. *Ibid.*, December 21, 29, 1719, January 7, 26, 1720.

158. "Liminality" as defined here is a state frequently considered in the works of the anthropologist Victor Turner. See particularly *The Ritual Process: Structure and Anti-Structure* (Chicago, 1969), *Celebration: Studies in Festivity and Ritual* (Washington, D.C., 1982), edited by Turner, and *Dramas, Fields, and Metaphors: Symbolic Action in Hu-*

man Society (Ithaca, N.Y., 1974). Turner's concept of liminality has been
broadened considerably by his disciples, and is used in this broadened
sense here.

159. *London Diary*, February 9, 1720.

160. For Byrd and Spotswood's reconciliation, see *ibid.*, April 29, 1719;
for the Council's effort to undermine Spotswood, see text and notes, below; for Spotswood's attempt to limit Byrd's jurisdiction, see Marambaud, *William Byrd*, 44; for Spotswood's description of Byrd as "implacable," see *ibid.*, 41.

161. "King's daughter," *London Diary*, August 27, 1720; "Secretary of
State," *ibid.*, January 2, 1721.

162. *Ibid.*, August 28, 1720.

163. *Ibid.*, December 24–27, 1720, February 18–26, March 9–13,
1721.

164. For sexual encounters with black women, see *ibid.*, December 9,
1720; for sexual encounters with white women, see *ibid.*, December 9,
1720, March 11, 13, 31, 1721.

165. *Ibid.*, April 9, February 27, 1721. For one example of Byrd's re-
solve to stop, see *ibid.*, December 27, 1720.

166. *Ibid.*, March 26, April 14, 1721.

167. *Ibid.*, December 2, 1720.

168. On the other man chosen agent, see *Correspondence*, I, 331; the
Council's suspicion was just a bit earlier, in May 1719 (*ibid.*, 324 n. 5).

169. *Ibid.*, 320–322, 324–326. For Byrd's quest for the "governorship,"
see note 64, above.

170. *Ibid.*, 326.

171. *London Diary*, February 6–9, 1720.

172. *Ibid.*, April 6, 9, 1720.

173. Byrd's abandonment of his ambitions to be an English gentleman,
and his gradual acceptance in and of his reduced role as a Virginia gentleman can be expressed in other, more specifically psychological or psy-
choanalytic, terms. The "reality therapy" of his failures, culminating in
the checks of 1718–1719, forced him to abandon his adolescent attempt
to integrate his ego-identity around his rigid model of "the English
gentleman" and in a sense liberated him from the paternal imperative (as
he saw it) to succeed in this role. He then began to reconstruct his identity as that of a Virginia gentleman, an effort in which he received immediate positive reinforcement and in which, by 1726 or so, he was successful. Further, he then had around him an abundance of mentors or role

models on whom to pattern thereafter a flexible, or metaphorical, version of his new identity as Virginia gentleman (see text and note 177, below). What happened, in short, was a shock followed by a successful reintegration of his personality around this new role, or identity. For background, see Erik Erikson, "The Problem of Ego Identity," *Journal of the American Psychoanalytical Association*, IV (1956), 144ff. Dr. Andrew Watson has helped greatly in expressing the event in these analytic terms.

In one sense what William Byrd was experiencing in his forties was only the integration of his personality around a role model he could manage, an event delayed since his adolescence by his long struggle with an unmanageable role, and in this sense only a delayed adolescence. Yet Byrd's crisis and resolution appears at the same time also to have been a heightened version of the "midlife crisis" commonly referred to in the psychological and popular literature of our day. In this case, a man in his forties was forced suddenly to do what men that age, today at least, are prone sooner or later to do, namely to reexamine his life and achievements and to come to terms with himself. Such a process also falls within the Eriksonian canon. In this perspective William Byrd seems, in the years after 1720, to have been compressing forty years of psychic development, from delayed adolescence to mature middle age, into as few as, say, ten years—if the further progress of his maturity described below can be said to have been completed by 1730—and so the late "maturity" depicted here and hereafter is a complex, a rich, and a condensed phenomenon. Not only did Byrd proceed rapidly from the onset of this crisis to learn from his peers in Virginia a "metaphorical," or living and flexible, concept of his new role as Virginia gentleman, but within fifteen years he would also reconcile himself to old age!

174. *London Diary*, February 24, 1720.

175. The elections are noted *ibid.*, August 25, 30, September 25, 1720.

176. For an account of this episode, see Marambaud, *William Byrd*, 44, and *London Diary*, December 19, 1720ff., including notes. Byrd's subsequent behavior is seen in *Correspondence* (1721–1725) and in Marambaud, *William Byrd*.

177. See text and note 25, above, for the origins and theory of the pathology which had led Byrd to the preceptual relationship to the world seen in his behavior up to 1719. A "preceptual" relationship is one in which obsessively fulfilling a rigid, highly specific action or set of actions is thought to enable one successfully to enact a role in society, in

Byrd's case that of a gentleman, while in fact cutting off nearly all flexible and reciprocal social relationships. "Precept" is here opposed to "metaphor," which term is used to describe the flexible and reciprocal relationships with other persons and with social reality which Byrd in fact evolved after 1719, and which characterize a healthy relationship with society. "Metaphor" is selected to describe this new behavior because in exercising such behavior Byrd was implicitly accepting that the concept of a gentleman was not a set of precepts but a metaphor for a state of being which could be acted out in social relationships flexibly and creatively, day by day. Hence, his new behaviors are the exercising of a metaphorical view of gentility, and in some of these behaviors he was to flex that metaphor—in essence to extend its limits—creatively.

178. *London Diary*, March 4, 1721.

179. See, for example, *ibid.*, March 5, May 1, 14, 1721.

180. See examples in the text and notes for 1717–1719 and for 1719–1721, above; these generalizations are based on such previous examples and on others from the *London Diary*, 1717–1721.

181. Again, a close look at the examples of anxiety, of sexual activity, of taking pills, of "putting myself in order" in the preceding notes will show how these signs of stress diminish after April 1720 only to mount to a peak between December 1720 and May 1721. Clearly, the final struggle with Spotswood, over Byrd's mandate from the Burgesses, interrupted Byrd's new calm and flexibility with a renewed surge of anxiety.

182. Assuming he received £400 for the agency and £200 per annum for the Council seat.

183. For Blair, see *Prose Works*, 42 n. 8, and Morton, *Colonial Virginia*. There are various accounts of Spotswood's removal, all inadequate; see Dodson, *Alexander Spotswood*, 226–276.

184. This and the following are from *Another Secret Diary*, 371–380 (see especially p. 371 n. 3).

185. The letters to "Charmante" are in *Correspondence*, I, 332–341 (see especially p. 332 n. 1). That Byrd never again exercised any of these witty genres has its possible exceptions (and certainly there was wit, and above all humor, in the newer genre he created later in his life), but that he now essentially abandoned those earlier genres can be seen in the introduction and table of contents (plus dating notes) to the writings printed at the back of *Another Secret Diary*; see also the judgment in Marambaud, *William Byrd*, 102.

186. *Another Secret Diary*, 379–380.

187. *Ibid.*, 276 n. 1, 379.

188. For Maria Taylor's background, and the Greek letter to her, see *Correspondence*, I, 348, including n. 1; subsequent letters suggest the uncertain fate of her dowry (*ibid.*, 503, 506).

189. *Ibid.*, 343–346.

190. *Ibid.*, 358.

191. *Ibid.*, 354.

192. *Ibid.*, 355–356. The myth-making process which Byrd finally took up at this point in his life had been begun by previously more committed Virginia gentlemen as early as 1699, and for the same purposes, namely to justify their status within a "purer" and therefore in a sense *more* civilized society than England's. See Carole Shammas, "English-Born and Creole Elites in Turn-of-the-Century Virginia," in *The Chesapeake in the Seventeenth Century: Essays on Anglo-American Society*, ed. Thad W. Tate and David L. Ammerman (Chapel Hill, N.C., 1979), 274–296. In my view, Shammas may partly misconstrue this process, which Byrd was to extend significantly (see text, below), as one of simple "replication" (p. 295). Plainly what Byrd was doing in this passage was flexing the metaphor of the gentleman-as-patriarch to show how much *stronger* it could be in the Virginia context than in England. It was therefore partly a new myth, one which ignored the Virginia gentry's massive dependence on tobacco, but was also more than a mere replication of an English metaphor. Similarly, Byrd's variations on the theme of gentility in his histories of the dividing line (see text, below), were a highly complex form of creative flexing of the metaphors of gentility in the New World context in a process of mythologizing the Virginia gentry's situation which was *of necessity* more than replication. Only such creative application of the metaphors of gentility saved the Virginians from the pressures and sterility of mere replication (see the conclusion, below), by giving them pride in that which made them different. It was a defensive, but also an effective process which Byrd embarked on here in 1726.

193. *Correspondence*, I, 356–358.

194. *Ibid.*, 371.

195. For background on Gooch, see volume II of Morton, *Colonial Virginia*.

196. Byrd's essay containing the above observations is published as *William Byrd's Natural History of Virginia: or, The Newly Discovered Eden*, ed. Richmond Croom Beatty and William J. Mulloy (Richmond, Va., 1940), 5. Byrd's unwillingness to recognize the growing power of the

Burgesses can be seen in his observation in May 1729 to Micajah Perry
that the Virginia Assembly (in this case plainly referring to the Burgesses) was the "very shaddow . . . of a Parliament" (*Correspondence*, I,
398). But this very occasion belied his claim, as he was writing of his fear
that the "shadow" Burgesses would submit to pressure from a rival family and force him to sell to the colony his land on the site of what later
became Richmond so the colony could establish a new town. Byrd held
off the Burgesses largely by starting the town himself. The entire transition to a more powerful House of Burgesses will be discussed in the conclusion, below.

197. See *The Secret History of the Line* in *Prose Works*, and Morton,
Colonial Virginia, II, 446–453; Byrd in fact created a "noble" order of
the turkey cock's beard (worn as a cockade) to parallel Spotswood's
"Knights of the Golden Horseshoe" of 1716 (see *Prose Works*, 116, 139),
though he dropped this from the second version, the *History of the Dividing Line*.

198. For the battle with the Perrys, see Price, "Excise Affair Revisited,"
in *England's Rise to Greatness*, ed. Baxter, 257–321; for Byrd's schemes,
see the *Correspondence* volumes for 1729–1740.

199. See previous discussion for the documentation of these points.

200. Again, see volume I of *Correspondence* as cited in notes 190 and
191, above.

201. Both are in *Prose Works*.

202. Marambaud, *William Byrd*, 120, identifies the report to the Board
of Trade; for the letter to Jane Pratt Taylor, see *Correspondence*, I, 384.
(Note that here again, as in a later letter to John Boyle [*ibid.*, 432], Byrd
still links provincial exile with death: "Fine ladys think of us unhappy
mortals that have the misfortune to be absent [from England], just as
they do of the dead." After 1730, such remarks were to cease.)

203. For the second letter to Jane Pratt Taylor, see *Correspondence*, I,
391–392. See note 216, below, for the subsequent letters here referred to
and for a closer look at the early stages of the genesis of Byrd's histories.

204. Daniel Defoe, *A Tour through the Whole Island of Great Britain*
(London, 1724–1727).

205. This reads between the lines of *Correspondence*, I, 355, 357–358,
361, 370, 372, 375, 381, 384.

206. Which, indeed, he had reaffirmed once again in his letter to Jane
Pratt Taylor of July 28, 1728, in saying "My stars . . . [have] denyd me

those smart qualitys [of invention] that might recommend me to her correspondence" (*ibid.*, 384–385).

207. *Prose Works*, 41.

208. *Ibid.*, 73.

209. On Firebrand's arrogance, see *ibid.*, 89; for Byrd's birthday meditation, see *ibid.*, 76; for examples of Steddy ministering to the men, see *ibid.*, 64, 69, 73–74; for Firebrand's abuse of the men, see *ibid.*, 71. Such examples persist as Byrd's manuscript continues.

210. These general themes so suffuse Byrd's *Secret History* that nearly every page offers examples, but Byrd himself sums it all up (*Prose Works*, 72). See also pp. 142–143, 149.

211. *Ibid.*, 67.

212. See *ibid.*, 27. I make this deduction from the available evidence, external and internal.

213. *Ibid.*, 239, 203.

214. *Ibid.*, 312, 320.

215. *Ibid.*, 184–185, 195, 204, 207, 212. Byrd's prose has been organized so that his comments on daily life, religion, and politics occur in that order and in one place. In general the sequence is close to that of his own comments on pp. 184–212.

216. Byrd was running the dividing line from March to April, and from September to November 1728; see *Prose Works* for Byrd's own dating in the histories. By May 28, 1729, he had decided to build the new "Westover" (*Correspondence*, I, 400; Marambaud, *William Byrd*, 52). As early as February 1729 he was beginning to acquire western lands along his route while running the line (*Correspondence*, I, 389–390, also 445–447, 448–452). The best commentary on the development of Byrd's western schemes is in Marambaud, *William Byrd*, 49–55. "Mixed people" and "Goths and Vandals" are from Byrd's 1736 *Natural History of Virginia*, xxi–xxii. On giving up his rooms, see Marambaud, *William Byrd*, 46, and a letter of May 28, 1729, in *Correspondence*, I, 399–400; at this point Byrd was having his books sent to Virginia and his London rooms rented out, but time proved that these actions in fact constituted a "giving up" of these rooms for all practical purposes, hence I hold with Marambaud on this point.

217. Marambaud, *William Byrd*, 54, and *Correspondence*, II, 530–531.

218. Marambaud, *William Byrd*, 119–121, mentions the process by which, beginning in 1728, Byrd's notes of the expedition grew into re-

ports, into the *Secret History* (perhaps by 1730–1733), and into the *History of the Dividing Line* (by 1737). Again (see text for notes 202 and 203, above), the process of fictionalizing or, rather, fabulizing, this experience can also be seen in its initial stages in *Correspondence*, from 1728 on; see, for example, pp. 374–375 (May 1728), pp. 387–388 (September 1728), pp. 391–392 (April 1729), pp. 393–397 (May 1729), pp. 404–405, 414–417 (June 1729). These early versions of the story were chiefly designed to impress family and influential friends in England. Only gradually, between 1729 and 1736, as the accounts in reports and letters expanded into the *Secret History* and then into the *History*, did Byrd use his expedition as the epitome of a larger civilizing process juxtaposed to the disorder of "Lubberland." Yet the theme of civilizing *is* there from the start, in 1728, but with nature as the opponent (*Correspondence*, I, 374). Sometime between 1728 and the writing and rewriting of the *Secret History* circa 1730–1735 (see Marambaud, *William Byrd*, 120), a feckless frontier society became the prime opponent of civilization, and it emerged openly as such in the *History of the Dividing Line*, written around 1736. It is impossible to know exactly when in the years 1729–1735 this theme actually came to dominate Byrd's thoughts, save that by 1736 it had and that by 1735 or 1736 he was insisting on Swiss settlers for his western lands. The earlier decisions to acquire large western holdings, to give up his rooms in London, and to build the new "Westover," made in 1728/1729 (see note 216, above), all strongly imply that Byrd had had an immediate reaction to the dangers and opportunities he had seen on the frontier; these early actions further imply that it simply took time, i.e., from 1729 to 1736, for this reaction to reach final literary form in the *History of the Dividing Line*. Similarly, it may have taken a like span of time to discover in Swiss settlers an alternative to the Scots-Irish.

219. Again, see notes 216 and 218, above, for reflections on the timing of the emergence of the vision in the years 1728–1736.

220. On Byrd's copies of Lucian and Homer, see *Writings of Colonel William Byrd*, ed. Bassett, appendix A; for Lucian, see *Oxford Companion to Classical Literature* (London, 1955), 246–247, *Oxford Classical Dictionary* (London, 1970), 621, and the Loeb Classical Library edition of Lucian's *Works*, edited by A. M. Harmon *et al.* (London, 1921–1967).

221. *Correspondence*, II, 494.

222. See *Prose Works*, 19–20, on Ruffin's edition of the *History*; for Ruffin's general despair, read between the lines of David Allmendinger's

rather too optimistic version of Ruffin's life, "The Early Career of Edmund Ruffin, 1810–1840," *VMHB*, XCIII (1985), 127–154; for the suicide of William Byrd III, see *Correspondence*, II, 610–613.

223. *Correspondence*, II, 443–597, documents these continuing themes in Byrd's later years, which are also recounted in Marambaud, *William Byrd*, 52–57 (who, however, misses Byrd's continuing effort to obtain German-Swiss settlers, reflected in *Correspondence*, II, 543).

224. *A Progress to the Mines* is in *Prose Works*, 337–378; for the visit to Spotswood, see *ibid.*, 355–366; for the pension request, see *Correspondence*, II, 549, 558.

225. *Correspondence*, II, 526–597.

226. *Another Secret Diary*; where dates are cited in the text, no footnote will be added. What follows in this paragraph is a judgment of tone based on this final diary.

227. Much of the "talking" can be seen in the long quotation from the diary in the text above. For "After dinner," see *Another Secret Diary*, January 8, 1741.

228. "Mary's birthday," *ibid.*, January 16, 1741. For one dream that Maria had died, see *ibid.*, December 20, 1740; for his dream that he would die, see *ibid.*, April 24, 1741.

229. "God's will be done," *ibid.*, April 24, 1741; "dumb creatures," *ibid.*, January 2, 1741.

230. As on January 24, 1741, *ibid.*

231. One should add "especially at home" to "avoided sexual play with his female slaves"; nonetheless, see *ibid.*, May 9, June 24, 1741.

232. For example, see the quotation in the text above, which is from *Another Secret Diary*, March 13–18, 1741.

233. For the Perrys, see Price, "Excise Affair Revisited," in *England's Rise to Greatness*, ed. Baxter, 302, 321. For Byrd's sale of land and slaves, see *Correspondence*, II, 484–485. For payment of his debts, see Marambaud, *William Byrd*, 55–56, who bases this largely on negative evidence. Yet the evidence of the late diary (*Another Secret Diary*) and of volume II of *Correspondence* is that any remaining debt was certainly not troublesome, which is also Wright's judgment (*Correspondence*, I, 200). For Byrd's succession to the presidency of the Council, see *ibid.*, II, 577, Marambaud, *William Byrd*, 56, and *London Diary*, 44–45. For Byrd's father as president of the Council, see *Correspondence*, I, 185.

234. See notes 25 and 177, above. The sources cited in these notes, above all George Herbert Mead and Peter Berger and Thomas Luckmann,

have been used to create a larger theory of unsuccessful/successful enculturation which seems to explain that evolution from "preceptual" to
"metaphoric" behavior seen so clearly in the course of Byrd's life. (The
precise meanings of these terms are given in note 177.) It is the implica-
tions of the theory, as it seems to be embodied in Byrd's evolution, which
are considered here.

Mead's work in particular, and this essay as an ultimate result of it, are
both outgrowths of the same movement for a humanistic sociology
which arose in W. I. Thomas and Florian Znaniecki's *The Polish Peasant
in Europe and America* (Chicago, 1918–1920) and found its theorist in
G. W. Allport, *The Use of Personal Documents in Psychological Science*
(New York, 1942). Allport especially spoke of using personal documents
to discover "the laws of social becoming." Mead's social psychology from
the same general place and time simply put personal development within
a social context on a theoretical level of discussion, in order to speculate
on "the laws of social becoming." Berger and Luckmann's version of
these "laws," as modified by Greg Dening (see note 25, above) seems to
fit William Byrd's case very well indeed. Byrd in turn illuminates from
within the process of social becoming as this school of thought has
sought to define that process over the years.

235. See notes 25, 177, and 234, above. "Maturity" is here defined as
the achievement of a flexible, reciprocal "metaphorical" relationship
with one's society and culture.

236. Greg Dening, "The Death of William Gooch" (unpublished seminar paper, Department of History, University of Melbourne, 1985); for
slaves, see Leslie Howard Owens, *This Species of Property: Slave Life
and Culture in the Old South* (New York, 1976).

237. For Pepys, see references to the difficulties Matthews, Stone, *et
al.* have had in dealing with Byrd's laconic diary, in the first pages of the
text, above; see also Bourcier, *Les journaux privés en Angleterre*, whose
final sentence leaves all English diaries before 1660 firmly in the shadow
of Samuel Pepys. Pepys's verbosity, and Boswell's later, have made it difficult for such scholars to deal with laconic diaries even though the latter
are a more usual form. Alan Macfarlane, *The Family Life of Ralph
Josselin, a Seventeenth-Century Clergyman: An Essay in Historical Anthropology* (Cambridge, 1970), is virtually alone in taking a deep look at
a half-laconic diary, or at what Macfarlane thought at the time was a
half-laconic diary.

238. Rhys Isaac, "Communication and Control: Family Government, Law, and the Feelings at Colonel Carter's Sabine Hall, Virginia, 1752–1778: Soundings in a Diary" (paper presented to the Shelby Cullom Davis Center Seminar, Princeton University, Princeton, N.J., 1982); and Rhys Isaac, "Description: A Diary and the Performances in It" (paper delivered to the History and Anthropology Seminar, Melbourne University, 1985).

239. Shomer Zwelling, "Robert Carter of Nomini Hall: The Seasons of a Man's Life" (unpublished paper on file, Research Department, Colonial Williamsburg Foundation, 1982).

240. Kenneth A. Lockridge, *Settlement and Unsettlement in Early America: The Crisis of Political Legitimacy before the Revolution* (Cambridge, 1981).

241. Some boys sent thus abroad never returned home, and some of these in a sense were casualties of this dilemma, such as Byrd nearly became himself, floating in limbo. See, for example, the potential cases in E. Alfred Jones, *American Members of the Inns of Court* (London, 1924), and see the histories of Richard Henry Lee and his brothers in Edmund Jennings Lee, ed., *Lee of Virginia, 1642–1892: Biographical and Genealogical Sketches of the Descendants of Colonel Richard Lee, with Brief Notices of the Related Families* (Philadelphia, 1895).

242. See *Correspondence*, II, 603–614, especially pp. 610–611 for the Robinson scandal.

243. Rhys Isaac, *The Transformation of Virginia, 1740–1790* (Chapel Hill, N.C., 1982).

244. Allmendinger, "Early Career of Edmund Ruffin," *VMHB*, XCIII (1985), 127–154.

245. See John C. Rainbolt, *From Prescription to Persuasion: Manipulation of Seventeenth Century Virginia Economy* (Port Washington, N.Y., 1974).

246. See Jack P. Greene, *The Quest for Power: The Lower Houses of Assembly in the Southern Royal Colonies, 1689–1776* (Chapel Hill, N.C., 1963), 28; see also, for example, the indexes of the county gentry's personal wealth and consumption, and the monopoly of high county offices by this group in Middlesex County in Darrett B. and Anita H. Rutman, *A Place in Time: Middlesex County, Virginia, 1650–1750* (New York, 1984).

247. Again, see Greene, "Opposition to Lieutenant Governor Spotswood," *VMHB*, LXX (1962), 35–42, and Greene's *Quest for Power*, 1–50,

for the general situation amplified in this and in the following remarks. See also the text and notes above, circa 1715, for the original narrative and other sources on the battle with Spotswood.

248. Greene, *Quest for Power*, 21–31; see also Jack P. Greene, "Society, Ideology, and Politics: An Analysis of the Political Culture of Mid-Eighteenth-Century Virginia," in *Society, Freedom, and Conscience: The American Revolution in Virginia, Massachusetts, and New York,* ed. Richard M. Jellison (New York, 1976), 19–35. For a grass-roots view of the way the gentry not only assumed, but also *shared* responsibility, see D. Alan Williams, "The Small Farmer in Eighteenth-Century Virginia Politics," *Agricultural History*, XLIII (1969), 91–101.

249. David John Mays, *Edmund Pendleton, 1721–1803: A Biography,* 2 vols. (Cambridge, Mass., 1952), I, 174–208. It took a much longer time for the gentry seated in the House of Burgesses to respond to a challenge from without which followed upon the heels of the Robinson affair. This was the coruscating attack on their moral "corruptions" and religious formalism led by the evangelical Baptists in the 1760s and 1770s, but in the end this challenge as well was met in a way satisfactory to all. See Isaac, *Transformation of Virginia.*

250. For "mimesis," see Jack P. Greene, "Search for Identity: An Interpretation of the Meaning of Selected Patterns of Social Response in Eighteenth-Century America," *Journal of Social History*, III (1970), 189–220. For extravagance, see T. H. Breen, *Tobacco Culture: The Mentality of the Great Tidewater Planters on the Eve of Revolution* (Princeton, N.J., 1985), 124–160.

251. Greene, *Quest for Power*, discusses this later period as well.

252. Richard R. Beeman, *Patrick Henry: A Biography* (New York, 1974).

253. *Selections from the Federalist: A Commentary on the Constitution of the United States, by Alexander Hamilton, James Madison, and John Jay,* ed. Henry Steele Commager (New York, 1949), reissued by AHM Publishing (Northbrook, Ill., 1982).

254. Edmund S. Morgan, *American Slavery, American Freedom: The Ordeal of Colonial Virginia* (New York, 1975).

255. Breen, *Tobacco Culture*, 124–160.

Index

recommended by Brathwait and Elyot, 23, 25

Death: dreams of, 75, 98, 101–102, 105, 148; in Virginia, 43–45, 64–66; of infant son, 55, 57–58

Debts: of planters to London merchants, 126, 149; of planters to treasury of Virginia, 159, 164; of WB II, 106, 121, 144, 149 (*see also* Parke, Daniel); of WB III, 158

Defoe, Daniel, 131

Dening, Greg, 171 n. 25

Des Bouverie, Sir Edward, 93–94

Diary: changes in character of, 127–128; general description, 1–12; origins of WB II's interest in, 22, 24, 32, 41–42. See also *Another Secret Diary; London Diary; Secret Diary*

Diet, 22–23, 65, 115

Distemper, 43

Dividing line. See *History of the Dividing Line; Secret History of the Line*

"Dr. Glysterio," 37

Dreams, 75, 104. *See also* Death, dreams of

Dryden, John, 37–39

Duke, Mrs. Henry, 105

Dunkellin, Lord, 91

Dunlop, Capt. Colin, 145

Dunn, Mrs., 67

Edenton, N.C., 138

Education. *See* Felsted School

Egmont, earl of. *See* Perceval, Sir John

Elections, WB II at, 112

Elyot, Sir Thomas, *The Boke Named the Governour*, 22–25, 49, 50, 142

Emotions, control sought by WB II, 6–9, 28–30, 41, 48, 51–52, 54–56, 147

English, daily reading in, 86, 114, 145

Eppes, Colonel, 105, 145

Eppes, Capt. Edmund, 145

Erikson, Erik, on identity, 185 n. 173

Evelyn, John, 8, 9

Exercise. *See* Dance

"Facetia," 34. *See also* Cromwell, Lady Betty

Federalist #10, 165

Felsted School, 11–25 *passim*, 171–172 n. 25, 172 n. 30

"Female Creed, The," 118, 127, 142

Filmer, Mary Horsmanden. *See* Byrd, Mary Horsmanden

"Firebrand," WB II's antithesis of gentleman, 132–136

Fontaine, Mr., 145

Fothergill, Robert, 9–10

French, learned at Felsted, 20

Friendships of WB II, 59–63, 114–116, 147, 148

Garraway's Coffeehouse, 85

Gentleman, seventeenth century, 20

Gentleman, eighteenth century, 6, 30, 32

Gentleman, English: concept